Me

Five Years from Now

Me

Five Years from Now

The Life-Planning Book You Write Yourself

Sheree Bykofsky

A Stonesong Press Book

HYPERION
New York

ISBN: 0-7868-8391-X

A Stonesong Press Book

Designed by Nancy Singer Olaguera

First Edition

10 9 8 7 6 5 4 3 2 1

Contents

Foreword by Richard Carlson, Ph.D. vii

The First Step: How to Get the Most from This Book xi

PART I: MY EMOTIONAL AND PHYSICAL HEALTH

1. Physical Condition and Health 3
2. Emotional and Psychological State 20
3. Religious and Spiritual Condition 34

PART II: MY FAMILY AND RELATIONSHIPS

1. Parents, Siblings, Children, Spouses, and Other Relatives 51
2. Boyfriends, Girlfriends, and Lovers 70
3. Friends 85
4. People I Must Deal With, Like It or Not 99

PART III: MY HOME AND COMMUNITY

1. Living Environment 113
2. Neighborhood 125
3. Hobbies and Leisure Activities 137

PART IV: MY WORK AND SCHOOL
1. Work 153
2. Financial Condition 164
3. School 178

PART V: HERE I AM AGAIN: BUILDING ON MY EXPERIENCE UP UNTIL NOW
1. What I've Learned About What's Possible for Me: A Checklist of Changes I've Made 193
2. The Pep Talk I Want to Give Myself: Things I Still Need to Work On 199
3. Moving Right Along: The Next Challenge 201

Foreword

Life doesn't have to be something that just "happens" to you. You have more of a say in your future than you might imagine.

The fact is that many people who feel they didn't wind up "where they wanted to be" had only the vaguest idea of where that place was. In my private practice and during my lectures I meet hundreds of people who feel they are somehow without direction—but admit they had no focus to begin with. In other words, they were lost from the very beginning because they had no practical idea where they were going.

Me: Five Years from Now is a wonderful book carefully structured to help you chart your path and achieve your goals. And your path will be illuminated by the ultimate expert in planning for your personal fulfillment—you.

This book is actually about more than planning. It deals with self-discovery, getting to know and trust the *only* person who is responsible for your happiness. You and you alone are in charge of determining the amount of fulfillment and gratification you receive from your life.

Let me first dispel some myths about the journey you're about to take. Effective life planning is not filling out a gigantic lifetime appointment book that marches you on a straight line to money, love, accomplishment, and prestige. If those things come, fine. But we all know friends and relatives who have achieved such goals and are sometimes left wondering, "Is that all there is?"

Realistically, a goal that is out of sync with your feelings, instincts, and philosophies is ultimately a hollow reward. So the first step in goal setting is to determine what you really want and adjust your priorities accordingly. For example, if success in business is your goal, you will find your life more purposeful if you redefine your business goals in terms of those basic values that are important to you. You may find that coupling service to community with the profits you justly deserve results in more service and more profits.

I believe that my most meaningful accomplishments come from within myself. The measure of our success should not come from external rewards—salary, awards, praise—but from personal fulfillment. Indeed, if you are on a planned path the external rewards will probably follow. Living fully is a way of *attracting* success. The more you give to life, the more you get back.

Your journey to fulfillment can start today—right now—and this book will enable you to write your own plan. *Me: Five Years from Now* helps you discover what you are all about. With pencil and paper, you learn a process that gets you reacquainted with the person deep inside, the "you" that may have been hidden behind doors you inadvertently shut and locked yourself. You'll evaluate your deeper goals and plan long- and short-term goals in accordance with your life's purpose.

Me: Five Years from Now uses an ingenious system to start the snowball effect of life-change. A series of small steps you plan by yourself leads to bigger and braver acts, and your new life gathers a momentum of its own. Finally, you fine-tune your actions. A self-evaluation system helps you change, reinforce, refocus, and stay on track.

As I hope you will soon discover, self-actualization is the key to *self*-help. While good advice is valuable, the ultimate provider of self-help is the self. The most successful and happy people are those who, when faced with adversity, find the solutions within themselves. "Self-actualized" people are confident in their abilities. They do not rely on others to set goals for them, and neither do they depend on external validation as a measure of success. They listen to their instincts and trust themselves.

Self-actualized people also refuse to have their spirits crushed by the past or by circumstances that cannot be changed. They break free from old relationships, say goodbye to blaming parents, spouses, or employers. They do what they can to overcome illness but do not let their illnesses control their psyches and their senses of self-worth. They believe in themselves and act in their own best interests.

Above all, they realize that happiness must come from inside. No amount of external validation can force an unhappy person to be happy. We all know of healthy and seemingly successful people who are paralyzed by depression. By the same token, if you choose to follow your own path, and create your own criteria for happiness, no amount of external adversity can "force" you to become unhappy.

Choose your path wisely, make sure it is really your path, and follow it. That is the fundamental message of *Me: Five Years from Now*. Keep an open mind, and stay alert to your dreams and higher goals. Look to the larger picture, and don't become obsessed with the details.

Remember what Mark Twain once wrote: You can't depend on your eyes when your imagination is out of focus.

—RICHARD CARLSON, PH.D.

The First Step

How to Get the Most from This Book

Most self-help books have one thing in common: They are somebody else's idea of what is good for someone like you. But is there really anyone else just like you? How far can we expect our powers of identification to extend?

Me: Five Years from Now is different because *you* are going to be the author. You are best equipped to recognize the unique and distinct areas of your life that you want to change. You have your own set of problems and limitations. You have very special likes and dislikes and goals and dreams and plans. This book is your personal tool. It can help you focus on yourself, examine your own particular sets of talents, possibilities, situations, limitations, and goals, and custom plan your own future. To make it easy for you, there is room to write in the book, and it was designed so that you can open it, read from it, and rework your plans for at least the next five years—or even longer.

The key to planning, changing, and coping is to learn how to determine what important facets of your life you have control over and then to decide to exert that control in a positive way—one step at a time.

The formula for instituting change is really very simple:

First you need to *focus* on your situation, your problems, concerns, and needs. The Focus section in each chapter will show you how to zero in on your likes and dislikes by making two columns and writing them down. You will then examine your lists and decide what's important to you and what you have the ability to change.

Next, you will *plan* by, first, thinking about your options. You will work at keeping the good things and eliminating as many of the bad things as you can. What compromises are you willing to make? What are the risks?

The third step is to *act*. This step will allow you to determine long- and short-term goals. You will think about what you can do today as a first step toward your long-term goals. Make up your mind to take at least one and up to three positive steps today toward achieving your goals. These can be little things, as simple as making an appointment, ordering a catalog, or changing the part in your hair. These are not chores. They are positive acts. They are part of the program that you have designed for yourself for the sole purpose of helping yourself.

The fourth step will be to *evaluate* your progress. This is done later, after you have embarked upon your plan. You will keep a record of what steps you have taken and all of the results—positive and negative. Then you can decide to chart a different course for yourself or continue as planned.

This book makes it easy for you to isolate different areas of your life so that you can focus on one set of plans at a time. Thus, it is divided into the following areas: health, relationships, home, and work. These larger areas are subdivided into smaller areas. You may find, however, that you want to work on an area of your life that is not exactly touched on in this book. In that case, you can use this technique to work through virtually any problem, difficult decision, or plan. After you become familiar with the book, you will see that the core of the technique is the list that you yourself make. You can use it to cope with loss, decide whether or not to get married or have a baby, decide whether or not to buy a house, plan for retirement, or expand your business.

In a nutshell, all you need to do is list the positive on the left and the negative on the right, circle what's important, examine your options, decide to change what you can, take action, and later evaluate. Take any situation; that is the idea.

For a brief example, here is how it might work for someone who has a business and is trying to come up with a five-year business plan. First she needs to ask herself a general question such as "What's my business like?" Then she needs to ask herself a series of specific questions. The answers should be written out in two lists, similar to the ones below:

THINGS ABOUT MY BUSINESS THAT I LIKE OR AM SATISFIED WITH:	THINGS ABOUT MY BUSINESS THAT I DON'T LIKE OR WOULD LIKE TO CHANGE:
I did better this year than last.	I'm not making as much $$ as I could.
I have two excellent employees.	Not everyone is pulling their weight.

THINGS ABOUT MY BUSINESS THAT I LIKE OR AM SATISFIED WITH:	THINGS ABOUT MY BUSINESS THAT I DON'T LIKE OR WOULD LIKE TO CHANGE:
I know more than the competition.	The competition is growing.
I have nice office space.	The office won't accommodate a growing business.
I'm making money on product X.	I'm losing money on product Y.
My business has a personal touch.	I'm too generous with my time and people take advantage.
The post office is right across the street.	Certain people are prejudiced against women in this business.

The list could go on and on; this is only a short example. Now the businessperson circles everything of importance on the list (which in this case may be everything but the fact that the post office is right across the street).

The next step is to examine the list to figure out how bleak the picture really is and to determine what things are in the businessperson's power to change. In this case, she decides the only thing she really has no control over is other people's prejudice. She decides that she does have the ability to improve several other areas of her business, though, and proceeds by making an "I could" list. Of all the possibilities she comes up with, she thinks about which possible actions are too risky or would result in too many negative changes. One possibility that she abandons, for example, is to close up the business. She does decide, however, to do the following things: replace a lazy employee; discontinue product Y and promote product X; hire an additional employee to screen phone calls; do a market analysis; mimic certain successful techniques of the competition; seek larger office space in the same neighborhood; and so on. Many of these things take time, but the businessperson decides to do the following things today:

Send a warning to the offending employee.

Look through the classifieds to see what office space is going for.

Place an ad in the classifieds for a new employee.

Tomorrow the businessperson will come in an hour earlier. Next week's plan will be to interview prospective employees. Later she will evaluate the results of the changes. That's all there is to it.

You can control the direction of your life. The world is going to change around you anyway. Why not exert a little positive control? All you have to do to make big things happen is a series of little things. And with focus and a plan, it's easy to identify and accomplish one or two small things each day if you know they have a purpose in the larger plan. For example, you might be intimidated by the idea of going back to school to improve your job. It may sound like too much. But if you've decided that it's a good idea, what's the harm of calling or writing a few schools and requesting their catalogs? When they arrive you can plan to look at them. If they appeal to you at that time, you can write for the applications and, perhaps, financial aid information. One thing at a time. That's all anyone can do. Still, the action is a step, and it keeps your mind on the goal you want to achieve.

Keep in mind, of course, that you don't have control over everything. You must assess your problems and plans and decide which things are in your complete or partial control and work on those. There are some things you can't change: certain physical features and disabilities, most things about other people, your need for sleep; but you can change your attitude, your job, your religion, and your environment. You may not be able to change your friends, but you can change who your friends are. You may not be able to change your boss, but you can change your job or some of the problems associated with your job. You can't change your landlord (unless you have legal grounds), but you can move.

Learning is enhanced by prior mental practice. If you can visualize a task before you do it, you will become proficient at the task faster than if you try to learn and do the task at the same time. Studies have shown, too, that people who imagine themselves as future successes perform better than those who imagine themselves as failures. If you imagine yourself as having achieved your goal, you will be more confident in going after it, are more likely to go after it, and will be better equipped to handle whatever it is you have attained. You will also have the satisfaction of knowing that your plan worked; you achieved your goal. This is true in all areas of your life.

Moreover, people with goals—and especially people with written goals—achieve much more than those with no goals. According to Forrest H. Patton, author of *Force of Persuasion*, "A study was made of alumni 10 years out of Harvard to find out how many were achieving their goals. An astounding 83 percent have no goals at all. Fourteen percent had specific goals, but they were not written down. Their average earnings were three times what those in the 83 percent group were earning. However, the three percent who had written goals were earning 10 times that of the 83 percent group."

Those who make an effort are successful—regardless of the results. If you've picked up this book and read this far, you're already on the road to improving your life over the next five years and beyond. Your next step is to pick an area that you would like to work on. Look for it in the table of contents. You will find that just as the different areas of your life overlap, so too will the table of contents. To really get the most from this book, use the sections together. For example, if you are having trouble at work, perhaps you will turn first to Part IV, Chapter 1 (Work). After going through the chapter, you may find that one of the worst things about your job is getting along with a particular coworker or your boss. You may then decide to use the chapter of the book that zeros in on relationships, Part II, Chapter 4 (People I Must Deal With, Like It or Not). Many of the chapters work well with each other, such as Work and Financial Condition. You may wish to use the section Husbands and Wives to examine your relationship with your live-in lover, or you may wish to use the chapter for examining family relationships to examine a relationship with a friend who is "like family." You'll know best which chapter will prove most useful at any given time.

You may want to use a separate notebook to make very long lists so that sometime in the future you can rethink certain areas of your life and see how your outlook has changed. But this book was designed to be written in; after all, you are the author of your life.

—SHEREE BYKOFSKY

I.

My Emotional and Physical Health

1. Physical Condition and Health
2. Emotional and Psychological State
3. Religious and Spiritual Condition

1. Physical Condition and Health

Focus

Do I consider myself healthy or unhealthy and in good or bad physical condition?

This is my medical history:

Just get it down on paper, and then we'll see what to do with it.

—Maxwell Perkins

This is my current state of health:

____

____

____

____

____

Make two lists side by side (see page 9). On the left, list those things about your health that you feel good about and are satisfied with. On the right, list the things about your health that trouble you or that you would like to improve. Think of everything, general and specific, important and trivial, but circle everything that is very important to you, because these are the things that will deserve special attention later.

Ask yourself any of the following questions that apply to you. If you like, jot down your answers right on the page. Then, later, transfer each answer to whichever list it fits; it's possible that some things will go on both lists.

Food, Weight, and Nutrition

Do I know what constitutes a healthy diet?

Do I eat a healthy diet?

What foods do I eat too much of?

What foods do I not eat enough of?

Do I overeat or undereat?

Do I have trouble losing or gaining weight?

What do I weigh and what would I like to weigh?

Do I feel healthy at my weight?

How do I feel after I eat?

General Health and Habits

Do I take any medication on a regular basis?

Do I still need these medications?

Am I addicted to anything?

Do I have any specific medical complaints right now?

Do I suffer from any chronic ailments?

Am I satisfied with the medical care I get?

Do I see the doctor too frequently or not frequently enough?

Do I see other practitioners, such as chiropractors, acupuncturists, nutritionists, etc., and if so, how do I feel about my alternative practitioners?

When was the last time I had a checkup?

Am I honest with myself about my health?

Am I honest with others who inquire about my health?

What are my bad health habits?

What are my good health habits?

Have I successfully broken any bad habits?

Have I tried unsuccessfully to break any bad habits?

Have I stopped pursuing my good habits?

Do I take care of my teeth?

How is my eyesight?

How is my hearing?

Do I suffer from frequent colds or other common ailments?

Do I pay too much or not enough attention to my health?

Do I feel I'm aging well?

EXERCISE

How is my energy level?

Am I able or better able to do most things that healthy people of my age can do?

What kind of exercise do I get?

Is exercise important to me?

Do I get enough exercise?

Do I enjoy my exercise?

Does exercise make me feel healthier?

What are my physical limitations?

Do I wish I could do things I used to be able to do?

Am I prevented from doing these things because I am "out of shape" or as a natural consequence of aging or because of some other physical limitation?

Do I have any physical limitations that prevent me from achieving my health goals, and if so, what are they?

Appearance

Do I like my body?

What do I like best about my appearance?

What things about my appearance bother me?

Do I pay too much or not enough attention to my body?

Do I sacrifice my health for the sake of my appearance? If so, how?

Do I sacrifice my health for any other reason (i.e., no time to floss my teeth, too expensive to visit the doctor, no health coverage)? If so, is it worth the sacrifice?

Health Programs

Do I enjoy taking care of my health or do I feel it's a bother?

What are five other specific things about my health that I

like and don't like?

Am I on the road to good health?

Do I do anything good for myself and my body on a regular basis (massage, facial, reflexology, etc.)?

Are my current health programs and habits long term or short term?

Do I want to be following the same programs and habits in five years?

Realistically, how do I see myself in terms of my health one year from now and five years from now?

Is my present course taking me there?

What other issues regarding my health do I want to explore?

People waste more time waiting for someone to take charge of their lives than they do in any other pursuit. Time is life. Time is all there is.

—GLORIA STEINEM

Things I Like About My Physical Health:	Things I Don't Like About My Physical Health:

List as many things as possible.

Now that you've made two lists, it's time to examine them. First of all, which is longer? Which is longer when you consider only those items that are circled (the things that are important to you)?

If the list of important things you don't like is much longer than the list of things you do like, you might then consider asking yourself whether or not you are really taking care of your health in a satisfactory manner. If the list of things you do like is much longer, you might then consider emphasizing maintenance over the next five years. In either case, it's time to work on changing whichever circled items on the list of things you don't like that are within your control to change.

So that's the next important question to ask yourself: Which items on the list of things I don't like are within my control to change? (It may help to examine the reasons these problems exist in the first place.)

Worry a little bit every day and in a lifetime you will lose a couple of years. If something is wrong, fix it if you can. But train yourself not to worry. Worry never fixes anything.

—MARY (MRS. ERNEST) HEMINGWAY

Plan

What are three things I can do to change each item on the list? List everything now. Later go back and think about the consequences and repercussions of each possible action. Think then, for example, if rectifying a problem will negatively affect any of the things on the other list, the things you do like about your health.

Things I Can Change About My Physical Health

A.

B.

Ways to Change Them

A. 1.

2.

3.

B. 1.

2.

3.

Possible Consequences

A. 1.

.

2.

3.

B. 1.

2.

3.

If at first you do succeed—try to hide your astonishment.

—Harry F. Banks

Following is a list of general and specific actions you may want to consider taking. Not everything on the list of suggestions will apply to you nor will they all be right for you. It is hoped, though, that the list will inspire you to come up with your own ideas about how to help yourself, plan for the future, and improve your life. Not forgetting to weigh the risks and consequences, could you see yourself taking any of these actions?

FOOD, WEIGHT, AND NUTRITION

I could improve my condition regarding food, weight, and nutrition by doing the following:

I could lose/gain ________ pounds.

I could have more fiber, more vegetables, less fat, less sugar, more fruit, less processed food, less salt, less coffee, more protein, less cholesterol, less soda, less alcohol, etc.

I could eat a more balanced diet.

I could eat more/less often.

I could join a weight reduction program.

I could eat more slowly.

I could read a book about dieting.

I could try some new recipes.

I could ____

____

General Health and Habits

I could improve my condition regarding my general health and habits by doing the following:

I could get a checkup

I could take a vacation.

I could get or change my health coverage.

I could get a massage.

I could see a specialist.

I could ask my friends to recommend doctors.

I could ____

____

Exercise

I could improve my condition regarding my exercise by doing the following:

I could join or use my health club.

I could walk up stairs instead of taking the elevator.

I could learn a new sport.

I could do yoga.

I could ride a bicycle.

I could dance.

I could combine activities, such as reading and exercising.

I could make an appointment with a personal trainer.

I could ____

____

APPEARANCE

I could improve my condition regarding my appearance by doing the following:

I could get a new haircut.

I could consider some cosmetic changes.

I could wear more flattering clothes.

I could buy a new perfume or cologne.

I could get a manicure or give myself one.

I could vacation at a spa.

I could ____

____

Health Programs

I could improve my condition regarding my health programs by doing the following:

I could ask people who have been successful how they did it.

I could ask the doctor to recommend programs to help with my bad habits or addictions.

I could try to locate an expert by asking people, by looking in the Yellow Pages, or by researching at the library.

I could read a book about natural cures.

I could do a workout video or TV workout program.

I could ____

____

Imagination is the beginning of creation. You imagine what you desire; you will what you imagine; and at last you create what you will.

—George Bernard Shaw

Now it's time to . . .

ACT

Look at your new list and ask yourself the following questions:

Which of these things could I do or start doing today?

Which of these things take time?

Are there any first steps I can take today to achieve any of my long-term goals? (For example, if you've decided that you may want to join a health club, today you could call a few or visit one.)

What are the general things I will try to do?

Tell yourself, I will do at least one new thing per day until I am satisfied with the state of my physical health. I will do everything in my power to work within my limitations. I will try to set realistic goals and will note each accomplishment. I will perceive myself as successful just for trying, and I will be gentle with myself if things do not turn out the way I expect. If I do not accomplish something I have set out to do, I will consider the possibility that I have tried to change something that is not within my power to change, and I will try to learn lessons that will help me in this and other areas of my life. I will not expect to change everything all at once but will take things one step at a time.

Things I Could Do Today:	Things That Take Time:

I will do the following things today:

2. Emotional and Psychological State

IMPORTANT NOTE: This section is not designed to help anyone with personality disorders, serious psychological ailments like schizophrenia, or profound depression. Such people may be well advised to seek professional care. If you are undergoing serious emotional distress such as that commonly caused by a death in the family or a divorce, you may also wish to seek professional care. This book may be useful as an adjunct for therapy but should not be a substitute for it.

Focus

The part of my life that causes me the most stress is:

My emotional and physical health (Part I)

My family and relationships (Part II)

My home and community (Part III)

My work and school (Part IV)

Other

I don't know

Everything

If you answered "everything," you may wish to consider seeking professional assistance. Continue in this section if your answer is "other" or "I don't know." Otherwise, go to the appropriate section in the book.

If I were describing myself in the third person as a character in a novel, this is what I would say:

____

____

____

____

This is how I'd like to be remembered when I'm gone:

____

____

____

____

This is how I think the person who knows me best would describe me:

Which is the more accurate description of me?

How would I like to change that person's perception of me?

How would most people describe me?

____

____

____

____

What would I like to change about that description?

____

____

____

____

Make two lists side by side (see page 27). On the left, list everything about yourself and your way of living that you like and that makes you feel good. On the right, list everything about yourself and your way of life that you don't like and that makes you feel bad. Think of everything, general and specific, important and trivial, but circle everything that is very important to you, because these are the things that will deserve special attention later.

Ask yourself any of the following questions that apply to you. If you like, jot down your answers right on the page. Then, later, transfer each answer to whichever list it fits; it's possible that some things will go on both lists.

My favorite time of day is _______ .

My most productive time of day is _______ .

When I wake up in the morning I usually feel _______ .

When I _______ I feel great.

When I _______ I feel great.

After I _______ I feel great.

After I _______ I feel great.

When I _______ I feel terrible.

When I _______ I feel terrible.

After I _______ I feel terrible.

After I _______ I feel terrible.

Some things that persistently trouble me are __________ .

Things I keep doing that I dislike doing are __________ .

Do I have a positive or a negative self-image?

What do I like best about myself?

What do I like least about myself?

My best talents are __________ .

I haven't had success at _______ .

I wish I could __________ .

I should face the fact that I'm no good at _______ .

People tell me I should change my _______ .

I get the most compliments on my _______ .

Do I like myself?

Do other people like me?

Do I like to help other people or do I tend to hurt them?

Do I feel basically understood or misunderstood?

Am I good at communicating my feelings?

Do I care what people think of me?

One character trait I would like to develop is _______ .

One character trait I would like to try to rid myself of is _______ .

What do I need more of in my life?

Do I usually know what's bothering me?

Do I think I'm always capable of figuring it out?

Do I wish I understood myself better?

Am I too emotional or not emotional enough?

Do I cry too much or not enough?

Do I worry too much?

Do I sleep well at night?

Do I feel guilty about things?

Do I blame myself for many things?

Am I too careful or reckless?

Am I too anything?

Do my emotions often get out of control?

Am I often afraid?

Am I often confused?

How do I generally deal with my problems?

Can I never/usually/always handle my own problems?

Am I afraid to get help, and, if so, why?

What things am I particularly proud of?

What are the things in my life that make me happiest?

What things about myself make me happiest?

Realistically, how do I see myself in terms of my emotional health one year from now and five years from now?

Is my present course taking me there?

What other issues concerning my emotional health do I want to explore?

The gift of fantasy has meant more to me than my talent for absorbing positive knowledge.

—ALBERT EINSTEIN

Things I Like About Myself and My Emotional Health:	Things I Don't Like About Myself and My Emotional Health:

List as many things as possible.

____________________	____________________
____________________	____________________
____________________	____________________
____________________	____________________
____________________	____________________
____________________	____________________
____________________	____________________
____________________	____________________
____________________	____________________
____________________	____________________
____________________	____________________
____________________	____________________
____________________	____________________

Now that you've made two lists, it's time to examine them. First of all, which is longer? Which is longer when you consider only those items that are circled (the things that are important to you)?

If the list of important things you don't like is much longer than the list of things you do like, you might then consider asking yourself whether or not you are really taking care of your emotional health in a satisfactory manner. If the list of things you do like is much longer, you might then consider emphasizing maintenance over the next five years. In either case, it's time to work on changing whichever circled items on the list of things you don't like that are within your control to change.

So that's the next important question to ask yourself: Which items on the list of things I don't like are within my control to change? (It may help to examine the reasons these problems exist in the first place.) Remember that it is hard or impossible to change other people, but even though there are limitations and risks, you do have at least some control to change yourself and your life. And do not lose sight of those things about your life that are important for you to keep.

Today my heart beat 103,389 times, my blood traveled 168,000 miles, I breathed 23,040 times, I inhaled 438 cubic feet of air, I spoke 4,800 words, I moved 750 major muscles, and I exercised 7,000,000 brain cells. I'm tired.

—Bob Hope

Plan

What are three things I can do to change each item on the list? List everything now. Later go back and think about the consequences and repercussions of each possible action. Think then, for example, if rectifying a problem will negatively affect any of the things on the other list, the things you do like about yourself and your life.

Things I Can Change About Myself

A.

B.

Ways to Change Them

A. 1.

2.

3.

B. 1.

2.

3.

Possible Consequences

A. 1.

2.

3.

Don't look back. Something may be gaining on you.

—SATCHEL PAIGE

B. 1.

2.

3.

Following is a list of general and specific actions you may want to consider taking. Not everything on the list of suggestions will apply to you nor will they all be right for you. It is hoped, though, that the list will inspire you to come up with your own ideas about how to help yourself, plan for the future, and improve your life. Not forgetting to weigh the risks and consequences, could you see yourself taking any of these actions?

I could try to be a better listener, more patient, more assertive, etc.

I could choose friends who are more supportive of me.

I could let my friends and family help me more.

I could be easier on myself.

I could stop closing myself off from people.

I could read a self-help book.

I could keep a journal.

I could ____

____

Now it's time to . . .

ACT

Look at your new list and ask yourself the following questions:

Which of these things could I do or start doing today?

Which of these things take time?

Are there any first steps I can take today to achieve any of my long-term goals? (For example, if you've decided that you want to be calmer, today you could buy a book about meditation.)

What are the general things I will try to do?

Tell yourself, I will do at least one new thing per day until I am satisfied with the state of my emotional health. I will do everything in my power to work within my limitations. I will try to set realistic goals and will note each accomplishment. I will perceive myself as successful just for trying, and I will be gentle with myself if things do not turn out the way I expect. If I do not accomplish something I have set out to do, I will consider the possibility that I have tried to change something that is not within my power to change, and I will try to learn lessons that will help me in this and other areas of my life. I will not expect to change everything all at once but will take things one step at a time.

Raise your sail one foot and you get ten feet of wind.

—CHINESE PROVERB

THINGS I COULD DO TODAY:	THINGS THAT TAKE TIME:

I WILL DO THE FOLLOWING THINGS TODAY:

3. Religious and Spiritual Condition

Focus

Is spirituality an important concept for me?

If yes, how do I celebrate my spirituality?

How do I think of myself in terms of religion and spirituality?

Make two lists side by side (see page 39). On the left, list those things about your religious and spiritual condition that you feel good about and are satisfied with. On the right, list the things about your religious and spiritual condition that trouble you or that you would like to improve. Think of everything, general and specific, important and trivial, but circle everything that is very important to you, because these are the things that will deserve special attention later.

Ask yourself any of the following questions that apply to you. If you like, jot down your answers right on the page. Then, later, transfer each answer to whichever list it fits; it's possible that some things will go on both lists.

Do I practice, observe, or commemorate my spirituality as often or as much as I would like to?

Do I practice what I believe?

If spirituality isn't a concern of mine, am I comfortable and guilt-free about this?

Can I explain my beliefs to family or friends who don't agree with my view or who are more or less spiritual?

Do I care to explain?

Do I believe in God?

What, if any, is my conception of God?

Do I believe in a being higher than myself?

Do I believe in an afterlife?

Is this something I think or care about?

Am I concerned about death?

Do my religious beliefs help me deal with fears, problems, questions, or important issues in my life?

Is there anything else that helps me cope with life?

Is "faith" an important concept to me?

Do I have a spiritual or religious role model?

Do I admire any others with opposing views? If so, how do I reconcile this?

Where do I think spirituality comes from (born with it, taught it, from parents, God, books, etc.)?

Has my concept of God changed over the years? If so, do I prefer my old concept or my new concept?

Is my concept of God a more traditional image, or is it altogether different?

Do I wish I believed in God?

Do I believe that people have the ability to decide their religious beliefs?

Do I believe that my religious beliefs are a condition of my cultural tradition?

Am I currently having a religious crisis?

How am I dealing with it?

Do I want other people to think the way I do? If so, everyone else or just the people I love? Why?

Do I insist that others believe what I believe? Why or why not?

If I have children, or if I plan to have children someday, do I (plan to) pass on my religious views to them?

How do/will I feel if they spurn my views?

Can I change their views?

Would I be happier if I reconsidered my position or if I stuck with it?

Would my children be happier if I reconsidered my position?

Does the question of marriage between people of different religions affect my life? If so, how?

Would I be happier if I reconsidered my opinion?

What would be the result if I changed my opinion?

Would others be happier if I reconsidered?

What would be the result for them if I did?

Have I been influenced by anyone who insisted that I believe what he/she believed? If so, what benefits and drawbacks have resulted?

Have I ever been angered by anyone who insisted I believe what he/she believed, and why?

How do my religious views help me or hurt me?

Do I want to change my religious views, and if so, how?

Do I believe that change is something within my control?

How would I be better off?

Does religion help everybody? If so, any particular religion?

Do I think that some religions are better than others or that some people are better than others because of their religion?

Do I discriminate against anyone because of their religious views? If so, how do I explain that?

What things about my religion should I or must I accept?

Are there other ways to cope with my problems besides turning to religion?

Would I be better off turning to religion or to a new religious practice to cope with my problems?

Are there other things about my religion that make me particularly happy, comfortable, calm, or satisfied?

Are there other things about my religion that make me particularly sad, confused, or nervous?

Realistically, how do I see myself in terms of my religion and spirituality one year from now and five years from now?

Is my present course taking me there?

What other issues concerning my spiritual condition do I want to explore?

Do one thing...imagine...see it and live it. Don't think it up laboriously, as if you were working out mental arithmetic. Just look at it, touch it, smell it, listen to it, turn yourself into it.

—TED HUGHES

Things About My Religion and Spirituality That I'm Happy or Satisfied With:	Things About My Religion and Spirituality That I'm Not Happy or Satisfied With:

List as many things as possible.

________________	________________
________________	________________
________________	________________
________________	________________
________________	________________
________________	________________
________________	________________
________________	________________
________________	________________
________________	________________
________________	________________
________________	________________

Now that you've made two lists, it's time to examine them. First of all, which is longer? Which is longer when you consider only those items that are circled (the things that are important to you)?

If the list of important things you don't like is much longer than the list of things you do like, you might then consider asking yourself whether or not you are really attending to your spiritual and religious needs in a satisfactory manner. If the list of things you do like is much longer, you might then consider emphasizing maintenance over the next five years. In either case, it's time to work on changing whichever circled items on the list of things you don't like that are within your control to change. It's in this section that the question of control for many people becomes particularly difficult to determine. What you yourself believe is ultimately the most important consideration here.

So that's the next important question to ask yourself: Which items on the list of things I don't like are within my control to change? (It may help to examine the reasons these problems exist in the first place.)

Old age isn't so bad when you consider the alternative.

—Maurice Chevalier

If you're not failing now and again, it's a sign you're playing it safe.

—WOODY ALLEN

PLAN

What are three things I can do to change each item on the list? List everything now. Later go back and think about the consequences and repercussions of each possible action. Think then, for example, if rectifying a problem will negatively affect any of the things on the other list, the things you do like about your spirituality.

Things I Can Change About My Religion and Spirituality

A.

B.

Ways to Change Them

A. 1.

2.

3.

B. 1.

2.

3.

Possible Consequences

A. 1.

2.

3.

B. 1.

2.

3.

How many cares one loses when one decides not to be something, but to be someone.

—GABRIELLE "COCO" CHANEL

Following is a list of general and specific actions you may want to consider taking. Not everything on the list of suggestions will apply to you nor will they all be right for you. It is hoped, though, that the list will inspire you to come up with your own ideas about how to help yourself, plan for the future, and improve your life. Not forgetting to weigh the risks and consequences, could you see yourself taking any of these actions?

I could seek or speak to a religious or spiritual advisor.

I could learn about various other religions.

I could do community service.

I could work on solving my problems through another outlet (such as psychotherapy, meditation, a weekend seminar, encounter group, support group, discussion group, etc.).

I could read books other than those pertaining to my specific religion.

I could visit an ashram, convent, synagogue, mosque, temple, school, or other religious institution or place of worship.

I could go to my place of worship more often.

I could celebrate more than one religion.

I could ____

____

Don't put off for tomorrow what you can do today, because if you enjoy it today you can do it again tomorrow.

—JAMES MICHENER

Now it's time to . . .

Act

Look at your new list and ask yourself the following questions:

Which of these things could I do or start doing today?

Which of these things take time?

Are there any first steps I can take today to achieve any of my long-term goals? (For example, if you've decided that you may want to learn more about your religion, today you could visit your local place of worship to find out about what classes they offer.)

What are the general things I will try to do?

Tell yourself, I will do at least one new thing per day until I am satisfied with my religious and spiritual condition. I will do everything in my power to work within my limitations. I will try to set realistic goals and will note each accomplishment. I will perceive myself as successful just for trying, and I will be gentle with myself if things do not turn out the way I expect. If I do not accomplish something I have set out to do, I will consider the possibility that I have tried to change something that is not within my power to change, and I will try to learn lessons that will help me in this and other areas of my life. I will not expect to change everything all at once but will take things one step at a time.

THINGS I COULD DO TODAY:	THINGS THAT TAKE TIME:

I WILL DO THE FOLLOWING THINGS TODAY:

Evaluate

I will keep a list here of all the things I've done and the results I've achieved:

Date	Step Taken	Results

Self-pity in its early stages is as snug as a feather mattress. Only when it hardens does it become uncomfortable.

—MAYA ANGELOU

II.

My Family and Relationships

1. Parents, Siblings, Children, Spouses, and Other Relatives
2. Boyfriends, Girlfriends, and Lovers
3. Friends
4. People I Must Deal With, Like It or Not

1. Parents, Siblings, Children, Spouses, and Other Relatives

NOTE: For each of the sections in this chapter, it will be helpful to concentrate on one person at a time.

FOCUS

Think of one of your parents, a sibling, your child, husband or wife, or other relative whose relationship with yourself you wish to examine or improve. Describe that person as if he or she were a character in a novel:

Now in general terms, describe your relationship with that person:

Our life always expresses the result of our dominant thoughts.

—SØREN KIERKEGAARD

Make two lists side by side (see page 62). On the left, list those things about your relationship that you feel good about and are satisfied with. On the right, list the things about that relationship that trouble you or that you would like to improve. Think of everything, general and specific, important and trivial, but circle everything that is very important to you, because these are the things that will deserve special attention later.

Ask yourself any of the following questions that apply to you. If you like, jot down your answers right on the page. Then, later, transfer each answer to whichever list it fits; it's possible that some things will go on both lists.

When I think about this person, what are the major feelings that come to mind?

Are those feelings recent or deep-rooted?

Is this a person I care about very much?

Is this a person who cares for me very much?

How much influence has this person exerted over my life?

In what ways has this person influenced my life?

Overall, has this person had a positive or negative influence?

Do I love this person?

Why do I think I love this person?

What are the qualities I like best in this person?

What are the qualities I like best about our relationship?

Do I feel our relationship entitles me to anything from this person, and if so, what?

What do I hope to derive from our relationship?

Do I derive those things?

Would I say our relationship is equal or one-sided?

Who puts more into our relationship, me or this person?

Is this relationship one of my priorities?

Does this relationship take a lot of time away from other relationships or priorities?

Do I want to put more into the relationship?

How important do I think I am to this person?

How would I change this person if I could?

How do I think this person would change me if he/she could?

Am I willing to change myself to please this person?

Do I care about pleasing this person?

Do I feel I owe this person anything, and if so, what?

Do I live with this person, and if so, is that a good thing for me?

Also, do I expect different things from this person because I live with him/her?

Do I respect and look up to this person?

Does this person respect and look up to me?

Does he/she rely on me, and if so, is it too much or not enough?

What are the problems with this relationship that have always bothered me?

What are the problems that have only begun to bother me recently?

Has our relationship changed for the better, for the worse, or has our relationship not changed too much over the years?

In what ways has our relationship changed over the years?

If this person weren't related to me, would I be his/her friend?

Does this person care if he/she annoys me?

Do I annoy this person? If so, do I annoy this person deliberately?

Do I think this person is justified in being annoyed?

Does this person help me in any general way?

What are some specific ways this person has helped me?

Have I helped him/her?

Do I feel comfortable talking to this person?

Are there subjects I deliberately avoid talking to this person about, and if so, why?

When I think about it, are those reasons valid?

Are we fairly open with each other?

Is it important for me to be intimate with this person?

Is this person interested enough in my problems?

Does this person pry too much or overly disturb my privacy?

Do I respect his/her privacy?

If I could tell this person anything in the world, what would it be?

If I would change anything, would it make our relationship better or worse?

Does this person listen when I talk to him/her?

Does this person respond in a way that satisfies me?

Do I listen well to what this person has to say?

Do I respond in a way that satisfies this person?

Do we argue very much?

Are those arguments enjoyable or troublesome?

Do we always argue about the same things, and if so, what?

Do we raise our voices more or less than we do with other people?

Has this person hurt me in any great way?

Was it deliberate or did he/she have good intentions?

Can I forgive him/her?

Has this person tried to make it up to me?

Have I hurt this person in any great way?

Did this person forgive me?

Do I forgive myself?

Do I see or talk to this person as much as I would like to?

Do I see or talk to this person too much?

What things do I hate about this person?

Have I told him/her?

Could I tell him/her?

Have we worked through the bad feelings?

If this person were no longer in my life, would I be sad or happy?

What would I miss?

What would I be glad about?

What would I be sorry I didn't tell him/her?

What would I be glad I didn't tell him/her?

Do I want this person to nurture me?

Do I want to be nurtured by this person? In what ways?

Does this person make me feel good or bad about myself?

Do I think this person understands me better or worse than other people?

Does this person open up new possibilities for me, and if so, what?

Would I say that this person is good or bad *to* me?

Would I say that this person is good or bad *for* me?

Husbands and Wives

Do I care about my spouse more than anyone in the world?

If I had it to do over today, would I marry my spouse?

What attracted me to my spouse initially?

Do those things still attract me?

What developed over time?

Is my spouse my best friend?

Are we tolerant of each other's needs?

Am I easy to live with, and why?

Is my spouse easy to live with, and why?

What are the qualities I like best and least in my spouse?

What are the qualities I like best and least about my marriage?

What do I expect to obtain from our marriage?

Do I get those things?

Did I use to get those things?

Would I say our relationship is equal or one-sided?

Do I want to put more into the marriage?

Do I wish he/she would put more into the marriage?

Do we share the housework?

Who does more of the housework?

Have we worked out our finances in a way that is satisfactory to us both?

Does one of us have more control over important decisions than the other?

Are we both happy with these arrangements?

How is our relationship like that of our parents?

How is it different?

Which similarities and differences am I happy about and which am I sorry about?

Do we get along with each other's family?

Is this a source of conflict?

Are we as intimate as I would like to be?

Does our sex life satisfy me?

How would I like to change it?

Am I satisfied with the quality of our conversations?

When was the last time we hugged and kissed?

Do I expect different things from my spouse than I do from other people?

Do I think my spouse expects too much from me?

Does my spouse listen when I talk to him/her?

Does he/she remember the important things I tell him/her?

Does he/she respond in a way that satisfies me?

Do I listen well to what my spouse has to say?

Do I remember things he/she tells me?

Do we have enough in common?

Do we fight fair or "hit below the belt"?

Does my spouse or do I use physical force when we fight?

Do we always argue about the same things, and if so, what?

Have I ever met anyone else I think I could have been happy being married to?

If marriage was a possibility, why didn't I marry that person?

Possible or not, what qualities did/does that other person have that my spouse lacks?

What qualities does my spouse have which that person lacks?

Does my spouse restrict me in any way, and if so, in what ways?

Do the restrictions make sense to me?

Does my spouse open up new possibilities for me, and if so, what?

Would I say my spouse is good or bad to me?

Would I say my spouse is good or bad for me?

Am I good to and good for my spouse?

Am I dependent upon my spouse or is my spouse dependent on me?

In what ways?

Do I like to be alone with my spouse?

In what situations do I enjoy my spouse most?

Do we have enough separate interests, involvements, and friends to keep us happy?

Do we have enough common interests, involvements, and friends to keep us happy?

Is this a source of conflict?

Do I always/usually/rarely prefer to spend my time with my spouse?

How much time would be just right?

Do we have enough fun together?

Am I jealous of my spouse?

Is my spouse jealous of me?

Are we supportive of or competitive with each other?

Can I pinpoint any feelings of guilt or hostility that come between us?

What other aspects of my marriage would I like to deal with or change?

Does my spouse get along well enough with the rest of my family?

Am I able to balance my marriage and my other family obligations?

Do I have or want to have children?

How does my spouse feel about having children?

Do we agree about how to rear children?

Do I put myself first, my spouse first, or my children first?

Who would I like to put first?

Are we a good team?

Are there issues associated with children that come between us?

What things about marriage are the most important to me?

Do I derive or do I anticipate deriving those things from our marriage?

Realistically, how do I see myself in terms of my marriage one year from now and five years from now?

Is my present course taking me there?

What other issues concerning my marriage do I want to explore?

GOOD THINGS ABOUT MY FAMILY RELATIONSHIPS OR MARRIAGE:	BAD THINGS ABOUT MY FAMILY RELATIONSHIPS OR MARRIAGE:

List as many things as possible.

Now that you've made two lists, it's time to examine them. First of all, which is longer? Which is longer when you consider only those items that are circled (the things that are important to you)?

It's unlikely you can change your family or spouse, but you can work on changing whichever circled items on the list of things you don't like that are within your control to change. So that's the next important question to ask yourself: Which items on the list of things I don't like are within my control to change? (It may help to examine the reasons these problems exist in the first place.)

If a person is to get the meaning of life he must learn to like the facts about himself—ugly as they may seem to his sentimental vanity—before he can learn the truth behind the facts. And the truth is never ugly.

—EUGENE O'NEILL

There are only two ways to live your life. One is as though nothing is a miracle. The other is as though everything is a miracle.

—ALBERT EINSTEIN

PLAN

What are three things I can do to change each item on the list? List everything now. Later go back and think about the consequences and repercussions of each possible action. Think then, for example, if rectifying a problem will negatively affect any of the things on the other list, the things you do like about your relationship.

Things I Can Change

A.

B.

Ways to Change Them

A. 1.

2.

3.

B. 1.

2.

3.

Possible Consequences

A. 1.

2.

3.

B. 1.

2.

3.

If you really know what things you want out of life, it's amazing how opportunities will come to enable you to carry them out.

—JOHN M. GODDARD

Following is a list of general and specific actions you may want to consider taking. Not everything on the list of suggestions will apply to you nor will they all be right for you. It is hoped, though, that the list will inspire you to come up with your own ideas about how to help yourself, plan for the future, and improve your life. Not forgetting to weigh the risks and consequences, could you see yourself taking any of these actions?

I could suggest we try something new together.

The next time I'm inclined to argue with this person, I could say something nice instead.

I could stop taking this person for granted.

I could try to put myself in the other person's shoes more.

I could forgive this person.

I could try to do more/less for this person.

I could write a letter to this person.

I could confide in this person more/less.

I could help this person with a problem.

I could ____

____

To know oneself, one should assert oneself.

—ALBERT CAMUS

Now it's time to . . .

ACT

Look at your new list and ask yourself the following questions:

Which of these things could I do or start doing today?

Which of these things take time?

Are there any first steps I can take today to achieve any of my long-term goals? (For example, if you've decided to spend more time together, today you could start making arrangements to make it happen.)

What are the general things I will try to do?

Tell yourself, I will do at least one new thing per day until I am satisfied with the state of my relationship(s). I will do everything in my power to work within my limitations. I will try to set realistic goals and will note each accomplishment. I will perceive myself as successful just for trying, and I will be gentle with myself if things do not turn out the way I expect. If I do not accomplish something I have set out to do, I will consider the possibility that I have tried to change something that is not within my power to change, and I will try to learn lessons that will help me in this and other areas of my life. I will not expect to change everything all at once but will take things one step at a time.

Things I Could Do Today:

Things That Take Time:

I will do the following things today:

2. Boyfriends, Girlfriends, and Lovers

Focus

Describe your ideal boyfriend/girlfriend:

If you have one, describe your boyfriend/girlfriend as if he or she were a character in a novel and make comparisons with your ideal (if you have several, just think about one at a time):

Now in general terms, describe your relationship with your boyfriend/girlfriend:

Make two lists side by side (see page 77). On the left, list those things about your love life and your relationship with your boyfriend/girlfriend(s) that you are happy about and satisfied with. On the right, list the things about your love life that trouble you or that you would like to improve. If you have more than one boyfriend/girlfriend, deal with only one at a time. You may use these questions to examine a relationship that is over; just think about the questions in the past tense. Think of everything, general and specific, important and trivial, but circle everything that is very important to you, because these are the things that will deserve special attention later.

Ask yourself any of the following questions that apply

to you. If you like, jot down your answers right on the page. Then, later, transfer each answer to whichever list it fits; it's possible that some things will go on both lists.

IF YOU DON'T HAVE A BOYFRIEND/GIRLFRIEND

Is it by choice that I don't have a boyfriend/girlfriend?

Why do I think I do not have a boyfriend/girlfriend?

What's good and what's bad about not having a boyfriend/girlfriend?

Am I comfortable meeting new people?

Do I put myself in situations that make it difficult or easy to meet new people?

Do I have a specific idea about the kind of person I would like to go out with?

Was I or am I afraid of being rejected, and why?

Is there any way that I could meet more people?

Do I have friends that could introduce me?

What qualities do I have that others may wish they had?

Are there any clubs or groups I might consider joining?

Are there things about having or not having a boyfriend/girlfriend that frighten me?

Do I expect that I will just meet someone someday, or do I think I will have to make it happen?

If You Have One or More Boyfriends/Girlfriends

When I think about my boyfriend/girlfriend, what are the major feelings that come to mind?

Are those feelings recent or have I felt them for a long time?

If recent, what precipitated the recent feelings?

Would I consider marrying my boyfriend/girlfriend, and why or why not?

Do I think our relationship is too serious or not serious enough?

What do I think marriage to this person would be like?

What attracted me to my boyfriend/girlfriend initially?

Do those things still attract me?

Is my boyfriend/girlfriend my best friend?

Are we tolerant of each other's needs?

Overall, has my boyfriend/girlfriend been a positive or negative influence on my life?

Do we love each other?

What do I like best about my boyfriend/girlfriend and our relationship?

What do I like least about my boyfriend/girlfriend and our relationship?

Do I expect anything from my boyfriend/girlfriend that he/she denies me?

Are my expectations reasonable?

Who puts more into our relationship, me or my boyfriend/girlfriend?

Do we share the costs and responsibilities in a way that pleases us both?

Do we get along with each other's family and friends?

How would I change my boyfriend/girlfriend if I could?

How would I change our relationship if I could?

How do I think my boyfriend/girlfriend would change me if he/she could?

Am I willing to change to please my boyfriend/girlfriend?

Do I expect different things from my boyfriend/girlfriend than I do from other people?

Do we rely on each other too much or not enough?

In what ways has our relationship changed since we met?

What are some specific ways we help each other?

Do I feel comfortable talking to my boyfriend/girlfriend?

Do we talk enough?

What issues concerning sex am I happy and unhappy about?

Are we as intimate as I would like to be?

Do we help each other when we have problems?

Do we respect each other's problems?

Do we listen to each other when we talk?

Do we annoy each other, and, if so, how?

Do we argue too much or not enough?

Do we fight fair or "hit below the belt"?

Do we always argue about the same things, and if so, what?

Has my boyfriend/girlfriend hurt me in any great way? If so, was it deliberate or did he/she have good intentions?

If I could put myself in my boyfriend/girlfriend's shoes, how would I describe his/her reason for hurting me?

Have I hurt my boyfriend/girlfriend in any great way?

Did I hurt my boyfriend/girlfriend deliberately or did I have good intentions?

Have we tried to make up with each other?

Do we see each other too much or not enough?

Does my boyfriend/girlfriend restrict me in any way, and if so, in what way?

Do we enhance each other's lives and help each other grow?

Are we too dependent on each other or not dependent enough?

Do we demand too much or too little of each other?

In what situations do we enjoy each other the most?

Do we have enough common and separate interests, involvements, and friends?

Do we have enough fun together?

What would I miss if we broke up?

What would I be glad about if we broke up?

How does this relationship compare to others I've had?

How does this relationship compare to the one I would most like?

What are the most important things to me about having a boyfriend/girlfriend?

Do I derive those things from our relationship?

Realistically, how do I see myself in terms of my love life one year from now and five years from now?

Is my present course taking me there?

What other issues concerning my love life do I want to explore?

You can have anything you want if you want it desperately enough. You must want it with an inner exuberance that erupts through the skin and joins the energy that created the world.

—SHEILAH GRAHAM

Things I Like About My Relationship with My Boyfriend/Girlfriend:	Things I Don't Like About My Relationship with My Boyfriend/Girlfriend:

List as many things as possible.

______________________	______________________
______________________	______________________
______________________	______________________
______________________	______________________
______________________	______________________
______________________	______________________
______________________	______________________
______________________	______________________
______________________	______________________
______________________	______________________
______________________	______________________
______________________	______________________
______________________	______________________

Now that you've made two lists, it's time to examine them. First of all, which is longer? Which is longer when you consider only those items that are circled (the things that are important to you)?

If the list of important things you don't like is much longer than the list of things you do like, you might then consider asking yourself whether or not you should change the status of your love life altogether. If the list of things you do like is much longer, you may want to concentrate instead on improving your current relationship(s).

In either case, it's time to work on changing whichever circled items on the list of things you don't like that are within your control to change. So that's the next important question to ask yourself: Which items on the list of things I don't like are within my control to change? (It may help to examine the reasons these problems exist in the first place.)

God grant me the serenity to accept the things I cannot change, the courage to change the things I can, and the wisdom to know the difference.

—REINHOLD NIEBUHR

Plan

What are three things I can do to change each item on the list? List everything now. Later go back and think about the consequences and repercussions of each possible action. Think then, for example, if rectifying a problem will negatively affect any of the things on the other list, the things you do like about your relationship.

Things I Can Change

A.

B.

Ways to Change Them

A. 1.

2.

3.

B. 1.

2.

3.

Possible Consequences

A. 1.

2.

3.

B. 1.

2.

3.

Following is a list of general and specific actions you may want to consider taking. Not everything on the list of suggestions will apply to you nor will they all be right for you. It is hoped, though, that the list will inspire you to come up with your own ideas about how to help yourself, plan for the future, and improve your life. Not forgetting to weigh the risks and consequences, could you see yourself taking any of these actions?

To Meet People

I could put an ad in or look through personal columns.

I could develop some new hobbies.

I could take a course on a subject that interests me.

I could ask someone for a date.

I could have a party.

I could go out more with my friends.

I could buy an interesting-looking magazine that might list events I could attend.

I could take a trip with a group.

I could ____

____

TO IMPROVE OR CHANGE A CURRENT RELATIONSHIP

I could write my boyfriend/girlfriend a letter.

I could tell my boyfriend/girlfriend what I've always wanted to say.

I could try to approach our relationship differently.

I could suggest we do something special together.

I could try to be more tolerant of my boyfriend/girlfriend.

I could spend more/less time with him/her.

I could forgive myself.

I could ask his/her side of the story.

I could try to improve the quality of our time together.

I could suggest we stop something that causes us trouble.

I could try to change the way I do something.

I could stop bringing up the past and work on the future.

I could stop trying to change him/her and try to change myself.

I could ____

____

Now it's time to . . .

Act

Look at your new list and ask yourself the following questions:

Which of these things could I do or start doing today?

Which of these things take time?

Are there any first steps I can take today to achieve any of my long-term goals? (For example, if you've decided to let someone know you like him or her, today you could offer a sincere compliment.)

What are the general things I will try to do?

Tell yourself, I will do at least one new thing per day until I am satisfied with the state of my relationship(s). I will do everything in my power to work within my limitations. I will try to set realistic goals and will note each accomplishment. I will perceive myself as successful just for trying, and I will be gentle with myself if things do not turn out the way I expect. If I do not accomplish something I have set out to do, I will consider the possibility that I have tried to change something that is not within my power to change, and I will try to learn lessons that will help me in this and other areas of my life. I will not expect to change everything all at once but will take things one step at a time.

THINGS I COULD DO TODAY:	THINGS THAT TAKE TIME:

I WILL DO THE FOLLOWING THINGS TODAY:

3. Friends

Focus

You may use this section to examine your friendships in general, or to look at one specific friendship. Think of one friend at a time.

Describe your friend as if he or she were a character in a novel:

Now in general terms, describe your friendship:

Make two lists side by side (see page 91). On the left, list those things about your friendship(s) that you are happy about and satisfied with. On the right, list the things about your friendship(s) that trouble you or that you would like to improve. You may use these questions to examine a friendship that is over; just think about the questions in the past tense. Think of everything, general and specific, important and trivial, but circle everything that is very important to you, because these are the things that will deserve special attention later.

Ask yourself any of the following questions that apply to you. If you like, jot down your answers right on the page. Then, later, transfer each answer to whichever list it fits; it's possible that some things will go on both lists.

Examining Yourself in Relation to Friends

Do I prefer to be alone, with one other person, or in groups?

Am I happy with the number of friends I have?

Am I happy, in general, with my friends?

Do I have trouble meeting people? If so, what may be the reasons?

Do I have trouble getting close to people? If so, what may be the reasons?

Do I tend to be jealous of or about my friends?

What do I expect from my friendships and do I get it?

Do I have fun with my friends?

Do I fight or argue a lot with my friends?

Do I want to change my friends in specific and general ways?

Do I want to change who my friends are?

Do I put myself in situations that make it difficult or easy to meet new people?

Do I prefer to be with new friends or old friends?

Do my different friends satisfy my different needs?

What do I like best and least about my friends?

What do I like best and least about having friends?

Are there any people I just don't want in my life anymore?

Why are they still here?

Examining Different Friendships

Examine only one friendship at a time.

Is this an old friend or a new friend?

When I think about my friend, what are the major feelings that come to mind?

Are those feelings recent or have I felt them for a long time?

If recent, what precipitated the recent feelings?

What are the qualities of this friendship that are like my other friendships?

What are the qualities of this friendship that are different from my other friendships?

Is this my best friend or one of my best friends?

Why do I think we became friends initially?

Are these things still true today?

How has our friendship changed or developed over time?

Are we tolerant of each other's needs?

In what ways has my friend influenced my life?

Overall, has my friend been a positive or negative influence?

Do we love each other? Why or why not?

What are the qualities I like best and least in my friend?

What are the qualities I like best and least about our friendship?

Who puts more into our friendship, me or my friend?

Does one of us have more control in making decisions than the other?

Are we both happy with these arrangements?

Do we get along with each other's family and friends?

Is jealousy an issue in our friendship?

How would we change each other if we could?

Am I willing to change myself to please my friend?

Would those changes please me?

Do I expect different things from my friend than I do from other people?

Is our relationship balanced or one-sided?

Has our friendship changed for the better, for the worse, or has our friendship not changed too much since we met?

Do we bother or annoy each other excessively?

Do we argue too much or not enough?

Do we always argue about the same things?

Do we help and comfort each other?

Are we comfortable talking to each other?

Are we as close as I would like to be?

When was the last time I hugged my friend, or is that something we don't do?

Do we respect each other's privacy or do we have no secrets?

Do we listen well to each other?

Do we remember the important things we tell each other?

Have we ever hurt each other?

How have we tried to make up with each other and have we been successful?

Do we see each other too much or not enough?

Do we bring out the best or the worst in each other?

Do we restrict each other in any way?

How do we help each other grow?

Are we good for each other?

Do we have enough separate and common interests, involvements, and friends?

What would I miss most if I no longer had this friend?

What would I be glad about?

Realistically, how do I see myself in terms of my friendship one year from now and five years from now?

Is my present course taking me there?

What other issues concerning my friendship do I want to explore?

I don't think of all the misery, but of the beauty that still remains....My advice is: Go outside, to the fields, enjoy nature and the sunshine, go out and try to recapture happiness in yourself and in God. Think of all the beauty that's still left in and around you and be happy!

—ANNE FRANK

Things I Like About My Friendship(s):	Things I Don't Like About My Friendship(s):

List as many things as possible.

____________________	____________________
____________________	____________________
____________________	____________________
____________________	____________________
____________________	____________________
____________________	____________________
____________________	____________________
____________________	____________________
____________________	____________________
____________________	____________________
____________________	____________________
____________________	____________________
____________________	____________________

Now that you've made two lists, it's time to examine them. First of all, which is longer? Which is longer when you consider only those items that are circled (the things that are important to you)?

If the list of important things you don't like is much longer than the list of things you do like, you might then consider asking yourself whether or not you should change the status of certain friendships altogether. If the list of things you do like is much longer, you may want to concentrate instead on improving your current friendship(s).

In either case, it's time to work on changing whichever circled items on the list of things you don't like that are within your control to change. So that's the next important question to ask yourself: Which items on the list of things I don't like are within my control to change? (It may help to examine the reasons these problems exist in the first place.)

The truth that many people never understand, until it is too late, is that the more you try to avoid suffering the more you suffer because smaller and more insignificant things begin to torture you in proportion to your fear of being hurt.

—THOMAS MERTON

PLAN

What are three things I can do to change each item on the list? List everything now. Later go back and think about the consequences and repercussions of each possible action. Think then, for example, if rectifying a problem will negatively affect any of the things on the other list, the things you do like about your friendship(s).

Things I Can Change

A.

B.

Ways to Change Them

A. 1.

2.

3.

B. 1.

2.

3.

Possible Consequences

A. 1.

2.

3.

B. 1.

2.

3.

Being a housewife and a mother is the biggest job in the world, but if it doesn't interest you, don't do it. . . . I would have made a terrible mother.

—KATHARINE HEPBURN

Following is a list of general and specific actions you may want to consider taking. Not everything on the list of suggestions will apply to you nor will they all be right for you. It is hoped, though, that the list will inspire you to come up with your own ideas about how to help yourself, plan for the future, and improve your life. Not forgetting to weigh the risks and consequences, could you see yourself taking any of these actions?

I could cultivate some new interests.

I could get back in touch with someone with whom I've lost touch.

I could spend more time with my friends.

I could help my friend with a problem.

I could forgive my friend.

I could be less hard on myself.

I could stop ________________________ .

I could pay more compliments.

I could invite someone to my home.

I could suggest we do something fun together.

I could try to be more independent.

I could cultivate a new attitude.

I could ____

____

If you expect perfection from people, your whole life is a series of disappointments, grumblings, and complaints. If, on the contrary, you pitch your expectations low, taking folks as the inefficient creatures which they are, you are frequently surprised by having them perform better than you had hoped.

—BRUCE BARTON

Now it's time to . . .

Act

Look at your new list and ask yourself the following questions:

Which of these things could I do or start doing today?

Which of these things take time?

Are there any first steps I can take today to achieve any of my long-term goals? (For example, if you've decided to preserve your old friendships because they are important to you, today you could call or write to someone you haven't seen in a long time.)

What are the general things I will try to do?

Tell yourself, I will do at least one new thing per day until I am satisfied with the state of my friendship(s). I will do everything in my power to work within my limitations. I will try to set realistic goals and will note each accomplishment. I will perceive myself as successful just for trying, and I will be gentle with myself if things do not turn out the way I expect. If I do not accomplish something I have set out to do, I will consider the possibility that I have tried to change something that is not within my power to change, and I will try to learn lessons that will help me in this and other areas of my life. I will not expect to change everything all at once but will take things one step at a time.

THINGS I COULD DO TODAY:	THINGS THAT TAKE TIME:

I WILL DO THE FOLLOWING THINGS TODAY:

4. People I Must Deal With, Like It or Not

Focus

This is a good place to deal with your feelings about and behavior toward coworkers, people you dislike, people who work for you, people for whom you work, neighbors, local store owners, and so on. Think of one person at a time.

Describe the person as if he or she were a character in a novel:

Now in general terms, describe your relationship with the person:

____

____

____

____

Whenever you want to marry someone, go have lunch with his ex-wife.

—SHELLEY WINTERS

Make two lists side by side (see page 103). On the left, list those things about your relationship that you feel good about and are satisfied with. On the right, list the things about the relationship that trouble you or that you would like to improve. Think of everything, general and specific, important and trivial, but circle everything that is very important to you, because these are the things that will deserve special attention later.

Ask yourself any of the following questions that apply to you. If you like, jot down your answers right on the page. Then, later, transfer each answer to whichever list it fits; it's possible that some things will go on both lists.

When I think about this person, what are the major feelings that come to mind?

Are those feelings recent or have I felt them for a long time?

If recent, what precipitated the recent feelings?

Do I deal with this person out of choice or is the relationship imposed upon me?

If I wanted to, could I sever this relationship?

Do I want to?

What is fine about this relationship?

What would I like to improve?

Could I be dealing with this person more effectively?

What do I like best and least about this person?

What do I like best and least about our relationship?

How do we please each other?

How are we fair or unfair with each other?

Do we deny each other things that the other expects?

Can we and do we tell each other how we please and displease each other?

Under what circumstances do we get along best?

Under what circumstances do we get along the worst?

Do we get what we expect from each other?

What are the qualities of this relationship that are like my other relationships?

What are the qualities of this relationship that are different from my other relationships?

How are we tolerant and intolerant of each other?

In what ways are we important to each other?

How would I change this person if I could?

How would I change our relationship if I could?

Do we have reasonable expectations of each other?

Do we argue too much or not enough?

What problems have we always had with each other?

What are the problems with our relationship that have only recently begun to bother me?

Do we listen well to each other and respond effectively?

Do we mostly agree or disagree about things?

Have we ever hurt each other?

Have we forgiven each other?

In what ways do we bring out the best or the worst in each other?

In what ways are we generally good or bad to each other?

If this person were no longer in my life, would I be sad or happy?

What would I miss?

What would I be glad about?

Realistically, how do I see myself in terms of this relationship one year from now and five years from now?

Is my present course taking me there?

What other issues concerning this relationship do I want to explore?

THINGS I LIKE ABOUT MY RELATIONSHIP:	THINGS I DON'T LIKE ABOUT MY RELATIONSHIP:

List as many things as possible.

______________________	______________________
______________________	______________________
______________________	______________________
______________________	______________________
______________________	______________________
______________________	______________________
______________________	______________________
______________________	______________________
______________________	______________________
______________________	______________________
______________________	______________________
______________________	______________________
______________________	______________________

Now that you've made two lists, it's time to examine them. First of all, which is longer? Which is longer when you consider only those items that are circled (the things that are important to you)?

If the list of important things you don't like is much longer than the list of things you do like, you might then consider asking yourself whether or not you should change the status of the relationship altogether. If the list of things you do like is much longer, you may want to concentrate instead on improving your current relationship(s).

In either case, it's time to work on changing whichever circled items on the list of things you don't like that are within your control to change. So that's the next important question to ask yourself: Which items on the list of things I don't like are within my control to change? (It may help to examine the reasons these problems exist in the first place.)

Learn how to pay compliments. Start with the members of your family, and you will find it will become easier later in life to compliment others. It's a great asset.

—LETITIA BALDRIGE

Plan

What are three things I can do to change each item on the list? List everything now. Later go back and think about the consequences and repercussions of each possible action. Think then, for example, if rectifying a problem will negatively affect any of the things on the other list, the things you do like about your relationship(s).

Things I Can Change

A.

B.

Ways to Change Them

A. 1.

2.

3.

B. 1.

2.

3

.

Possible Consequences

A. 1.

2.

3.

B. 1.

2.

3.

Following is a list of general and specific actions you may want to consider taking. Not everything on the list of suggestions will apply to you nor will they all be right for you. It is hoped, though, that the list will inspire you to come up with your own ideas about how to help yourself, plan for the future, and improve your life. Not forgetting to weigh the risks and consequences, could you see yourself taking any of these actions?

I could be more assertive.

I could try to communicate my feelings and needs more clearly.

I could try to approach this relationship differently.

I could try harder to see his/her point of view.

I could be more or less demanding.

I could let the person know what I like and don't like about him/her.

I could try to clear the air.

I could turn the other cheek.

I could try a new tactic for dealing with the person.

I could prioritize my grievances ("pick my fights").

I could ____

____

Now it's time to . . .

Act

Look at your new list and ask yourself the following questions:

Which of these things could I do or start doing today?

Which of these things take time?

Are there any first steps I can take today to achieve any of my long-term goals? (For example, if you've decided to find a new employee, today you could ask around for recommendations.)

What are the general things I will try to do?

Tell yourself, I will do at least one new thing per day until I am satisfied with the state of my relationship(s). I will do everything in my power to work within my limitations. I will try to set realistic goals and will note each accomplishment. I will perceive myself as successful just for trying, and I will be gentle with myself if things do not turn out the way I expect. If I do not accomplish something I have set out to do, I will consider the possibility that I have tried to change something that is not within my power to change, and I will try to learn lessons that will help me in this and other areas of my life. I will not expect to change everything all at once but will take things one step at a time.

Things I Could Do Today:	Things That Take Time:

I will do the following things today:

EVALUATE

I will keep a list here of all the things I've done and the results I've achieved:

DATE	STEP TAKEN	RESULTS

III.

My Home and Community

1. Living Environment
2. Neighborhood
3. Hobbies and Leisure Activities

1. Living Environment

Focus

This is how someone who's never been here might describe my living environment (the people I live with and the interior of my home—the neighborhood is dealt with in the next section):

This is how I would describe my living environment:

To escape criticism—do nothing, be nothing.

—ELBERT HUBBARD

Make two lists side by side (see page 117). On the left, list those things about your living environment that you feel good about and are satisfied with. On the right, list the things about your home that trouble you or that you would like to improve. Think of everything, general and specific, important and trivial, but circle everything that is very important to you, because these are the things that will deserve special attention later.

Ask yourself any of the following questions that apply to you. If you like, jot down your answers right on the page. Then, later, transfer each answer to whichever list it fits; it's possible that some things will go on both lists.

What are the main problems about my home that always bother me?

What do I like best about living here?

What is the most important thing about "home" to me?

Do I use all of the rooms of my home?

Specifically and generally, how do I feel about each room?

Where do I spend most of my time?

Is there anything I keep tripping over?

Does anything make me feel bad when I look at it?

Which pieces of furniture and furnishings do I like the best and least?

Is my home decorated and furnished in the way that appeals to me the most?

Would certain rooms look better if I moved around the furniture?

Does anything about my home embarrass me when people come to visit?

Do people who live here complain about certain aspects of my home?

Who has more control over the environment, them or me?

What things are in need of repair?

Do I like the colors of my walls and the look of my floor?

Can I afford to make the changes I envision?

Do I like clutter or a simple, minimalist look?

Do I keep anything just for nostalgia?

Do I want my home to reflect me and does it?

Do I hold on to things too long?

Do I throw things away and then have regrets?

Do I enjoy getting rid of things?

Are there many things that I never look at or use?

Am I handy enough to make changes instead of hiring outsiders or buying new things?

Are there any large purchases I want to save up for?

How do my living needs differ from others who live here?

What compromises can we make to live harmoniously?

Do I have a space that is all my own, that everyone respects?

Is the same true for everyone who lives here?

Is there enough community space here, where people can interact well?

Am I basically happy or unhappy with the people I live with?

Do I have or want pets?

What changes should I make or do I want to make to accommodate adults or children or pets who live here?

Do people like to visit me?

Do I like when people visit?

Is it important to me if my home is neat and clean and do I keep it that way?

Do I feel the housework is shared fairly or to everyone's satisfaction?

Are there other people's homes I like better than mine? If so, what things do I like better about their homes?

Do I feel safe at home?

Do I feel comfortable?

If I moved or made changes, what would I like to remain the same about my living situation?

Realistically, how do I see myself in terms of my home one year from now and five years from now?

Is my present course taking me there?

What other issues regarding my home do I want to explore?

Things I Like About My Home:	Things I Don't Like About My Home:

List as many things as possible.

Now that you've made two lists, it's time to examine them. First of all, which is longer? Which is longer when you consider only those items that are circled (the things that are important to you)?

If the list of important things you don't like is much longer than the list of things you do like, you might then consider asking yourself whether or not you should change your living environment altogether. In either case, it's time to work on changing whichever circled items on the list of things you don't like that are within your control to change.

So that's the next important question to ask yourself: Which items on the list of things I don't like are within my control to change? (It may help to examine the reasons these problems exist in the first place.)

No problem is so big or so complicated that it can't be run away from.

—Linus, Peanuts cartoon character

Plan

What are three things I can do to change each item on the list? List everything now. Later go back and think about the consequences and repercussions of each possible action. Think then, for example, if rectifying a problem will negatively affect any of the things on the other list, the things you do like about your home.

Things I Can Change

A.

B.

Ways to Change Them

A. 1.

2.

3.

B. 1.

2.

3.

Possible Consequences

A. 1.

2.

3.

The way you overcome shyness is to become so wrapped up in something you forget to be afraid.

—Lady Bird Johnson

B. 1.

2.

3.

The greatest thing in family life is to take a hint when a hint is intended—and not to take a hint when a hint isn't intended.

—ROBERT FROST

Following is a list of general and specific actions you may want to consider taking. Not everything on the list of suggestions will apply to you nor will they all be right for you. It is hoped, though, that the list will inspire you to come up with your own ideas about how to help yourself, plan for the future, and improve your life. Not forgetting to weigh the risks and consequences, could you see yourself taking any of these actions?

I could rearrange my furniture.

I could do a spring cleaning.

I could buy or save for something new.

I could hire a cleaning person, if only occasionally.

I could redecorate by myself or with an expert or friend.

I could change the use of one of the rooms or areas.

I could paint or wallpaper my walls.

I could refinish the furniture.

I could organize my files.

I could get or give away a pet.

I could ____

____

Trouble is part of your life, and if you don't share it, you don't give the person who loves you a chance to love you enough.

—DINAH SHORE

Now it's time to . . .

Act

Look at your new list and ask yourself the following questions:

Which of these things could I do or start doing today?

Which of these things take time?

Are there any first steps I can take today to achieve any of my long-term goals? (For example, if you've decided to renovate your bathroom, today you could start getting estimates on what it would cost and make a list of what you'd like in your new bathroom.)

What are the general things I will try to do?

Tell yourself, I will do at least one new thing per day until I am satisfied with the state of my living environment. I will do everything in my power to work within my limitations. I will try to set realistic goals and will note each accomplishment. I will perceive myself as successful just for trying, and I will be gentle with myself if things do not turn out the way I expect. If I do not accomplish something I have set out to do, I will consider the possibility that I have tried to change something that is not within my power to change, and I will try to learn lessons that will help me in this and other areas of my life. I will not expect to change everything all at once but will take things one step at a time.

Things I Could Do Today:	Things That Take Time:

I will do the following things today:

2. Neighborhood

FOCUS

This is how I would describe my neighborhood to someone who was thinking about moving here:

____

____

____

____

This is how I feel about my neighborhood:

____

____

____

____

While all deception requires secrecy, all secrecy is not meant to deceive.

—SISSELA BOK

Make two lists side by side (see page 129). On the left, list those things about your neighborhood that you feel good about and are satisfied with. On the right, list the things about your neighborhood that trouble you or that you would like to improve. Think of everything, general and specific, important and trivial, but circle everything that is very important to you, because these are the things that will deserve special attention later.

Ask yourself any of the following questions that apply to you. If you like, jot down your answers right on the page. Then, later, transfer each answer to whichever list it fits; it's possible that some things will go on both lists.

What are the main problems about my neighborhood that always bother me?

Where would I live if I could live anywhere in the world?

Why don't I live there?

Compared to my ideal place, what is the same about living where I am?

What is different about living where I am?

What are the best and worst features of this neighborhood?

Do I prefer the country or the city or the suburbs?

What are the most important features of a neighborhood to me, and does my neighborhood provide them?

Do I prefer to live in a house, condo, co-op, rental apartment, or other?

Do I know and get along with my neighbors?

What facilities are nearby that I use?

What facilities do I wish were nearby?

Do I have enough or too many family and friends nearby?

Is my neighborhood pretty enough for me?

Do I feel like I'm part of my neighborhood?

Do I belong to any neighborhood clubs or organizations?

Do I participate in community politics?

Do my politics match those of my community?

Do I want my neighbors to be like me? Are they?

How would I like them to be different?

Do I feel at home in this neighborhood?

Do I feel safe in this neighborhood?

Do the people I live with feel safe and at home in this neighborhood?

Is there anything very wrong about this neighborhood?

Keep changing. When you're through changing, you're through.

—Bruce Barton

Is it easy to get to work?

Can I afford to live somewhere that I would like better?

Did I ever live anywhere I preferred more? If so, what did I prefer about that place?

Have I lived here too long or not long enough?

Does living in this neighborhood make it easy or hard to do things I like or need to do (such as shopping)?

Do I wish my neighborhood would change and how?

Do I need a change?

Do I and the people I live with differ in our neighborhood needs?

Where would I like to be living one year from now and five years from now?

Is my present course taking me there?

What other issues regarding my neighborhood do I want to explore?

A lonely person cannot, then, wait for friends to assemble around and take care of him. Friendship, for each of us, begins with reaching out....When a person asks that age-old question, "What can I do about my terrible loneliness?" the best answer is still, "Do something for somebody else."

—ANN LANDERS, CREDITING DR. EUGENE KENNEDY

Things I Like About My Neighborhood:	Things I Don't Like About My Neighborhood:

List as many things as possible.

Now that you've made two lists, it's time to examine them. First of all, which is longer? Which is longer when you consider only those items that are circled (the things that are important to you)?

If the list of important things you don't like is much longer than the list of things you do like, you might then consider moving. In either case, it's time to work on changing whichever circled items on the list of things you don't like that are within your control to change.

So that's the next important question to ask yourself: Which items on the list of things I don't like are within my control to change? (It may help to examine the reasons these problems exist in the first place.)

People change and forget to tell each other.

—LILLIAN HELLMAN

Plan

What are three things I can do to change each item on the list? List everything now. Later go back and think about the consequences and repercussions of each possible action. Think then, for example, if rectifying a problem will negatively affect any of the things on the other list, the things you do like about your neighborhood.

Things I Can Change

A.

B.

Ways to Change Them

A. 1.

2.

3.

B. 1.

2.

3.

Possible Consequences

A. 1.

2.

3.

B. 1.

2.

3.

A tough lesson in life that one has to learn is that not everybody wishes you well.

—Dan Rather

Following is a list of general and specific actions you may want to consider taking. Not everything on the list of suggestions will apply to you nor will they all be right for you. It is hoped, though, that the list will inspire you to come up with your own ideas about how to help yourself, plan for the future, and improve your life. Not forgetting to weigh the risks and consequences, could you see yourself taking any of these actions?

I could shop for a mortgage or a better mortgage.

I could see a real estate broker about buying or selling.

I could paint my house.

I could attend a local meeting.

I could start using some of the local facilities.

I could read a book about home buying.

I could do something to beautify the neighborhood.

I could welcome my new neighbor.

I could initiate a block cleanup or block party.

I could form a car pool.

I could ______________________________

____

I'd like to reverse a traditional piece of commencement-time advice. You know it well, it goes: "Make no little plans." Instead, I'd like to say this: Make no little enemies—people with whom you differ for some petty, insignificant, personal reason. Instead, I would urge you to cultivate "mighty opposites"—people with whom you disagree on big issues, with whom you will fight to the end over fundamental convictions. And that fight, I can assure you, will be good for you and your opponent.

—THOMAS J. WATSON, JR.

Now it's time to . . .

Act

Look at your new list and ask yourself the following questions:

Which of these things could I do or start doing today?

Which of these things take time?

Are there any first steps I can take today to achieve any of my long-term goals? (For example, if you've decided to find out why your cousin loves living in Albuquerque, you could start making plans to visit today by calling or writing to her or by finding out the price of an airline ticket to get there.)

What are the general things I will try to do?

Tell yourself, I will do at least one new thing per day until I am satisfied with my neighborhood. I will do everything in my power to work within my limitations. I will try to set realistic goals and will note each accomplishment. I will perceive myself as successful just for trying, and I will be gentle with myself if things do not turn out the way I expect. If I do not accomplish something I have set out to do, I will consider the possibility that I have tried to change something that is not within my power to change, and I will try to learn lessons that will help me in this and other areas of my life. I will not expect to change everything all at once but will take things one step at a time.

Things I Could Do Today:	Things That Take Time:

I will do the following things today:

3. Hobbies and Leisure Activities

Focus

If someone asked me what my hobbies and leisure activities were, I would tell them this:

This is how I feel about my current hobbies and leisure time:

If fifty million people say a foolish thing, it is still a foolish thing.

—Anatole France

Make two lists side by side (see page 141). On the left, list all of those things about your hobbies and leisure activities that you feel good about and are satisfied with. On the right, list the things about your hobbies and leisure activities that trouble you or that you would like to improve. Think of everything, general and specific, important and trivial, but circle everything that is very important to you, because these are the things that will deserve special attention later.

Ask yourself any of the following questions that apply to you. If you like, jot down your answers right on the page. Then, later, transfer each answer to whichever list it fits; it's possible that some things will go on both lists.

What do I spend most of my leisure time doing?

What do I enjoy about my hobbies and leisure activities?

What do I not enjoy about them?

Do I have enough leisure time to spend doing what I enjoy doing?

What are some other people's hobbies that appeal to me?

Ideally, how would I like to spend my leisure time?

Do my leisure activities suit my talents and temperament?

Do I like my hobbies to be fun or to give me a sense of achievement or both?

Do I like competition?

Do I prefer solitary hobbies or ones that involve another person or many other people?

Is there anything I'm particularly knowledgeable about or good at?

Would I enjoy a new hobby associated with that knowledge or skill?

Do I collect anything or would I enjoy being a collector?

Do I use hobbies to meet people or get away from them?

Do I think there may be a hobby that I'd enjoy that I've never tried?

Do I have the necessary skills or would I have to acquire them?

Do I enjoy trying new things or prefer what's tried and true?

Do I like creating things?

Have I given up any old hobbies? If so, do I miss them?

Is there a good reason why I don't do them anymore?

Do I have a project that I've always wanted to get around to that I've never gotten around to?

Is it possible that I don't really want to do it?

Are hobbies important to me or a waste of time?

Are there any risks associated with my current leisure activities?

Are there any risks associated with the leisure activities I contemplate doing?

Are the activities worth the risks?

What obstacles are keeping me from doing the leisure activities that I would enjoy most?

Am I in or would I like to belong to any clubs or organizations?

Would I or do I enjoy doing any volunteer work or other community activity?

Do I pursue cultural activities in a way that suits me?

Do I like to read, and if so, do I read as much as I would like?

What subjects would I like to know more about?

Have I taken any classes since I went to school, and were they satisfying?

Am I satisfied with my social life?

Are there pressures or problems interfering with my enjoyment of my leisure time?

Would I like to turn one or more of my leisure activities into a business?

Do I intend to be pursuing the same hobbies and leisure activities one year or five years from now?

Are my hobbies and leisure time activities associated with any goals that I would like to achieve over the next five years?

Realistically, where would I like to be in terms of my hobbies and leisure time one year and five years from now?

Is my present course taking me there?

What other issues regarding my hobbies and leisure time do I want to explore?

Things I Like About My Hobbies and Leisure Time:	Things I Don't Like About My Hobbies and Leisure Time:

List as many things as possible.

Now that you've made two lists, it's time to examine them. First of all, which is longer? Which is longer when you consider only those items that are circled (the things that are important to you)?

If the list of important things you don't like is much longer than the list of things you do like, you might then consider some new hobbies. If the list of things you do like is much longer, you should probably concentrate instead on continuing your old hobbies. In either case, it's time to work on changing whichever circled items on the list of things you don't like that are within your control to change.

So that's the next important question to ask yourself: Which items on the list of things I don't like are within my control to change? (It may help to examine the reasons these problems exist in the first place.)

The danger of the past was that men became slaves. The danger of the future is that men may become robots.

—Erich Fromm

PLAN

What are three things I can do to change each item on the list? List everything now. Later go back and think about the consequences and repercussions of each possible action. Think then, for example, if rectifying a problem will negatively affect any of the things on the other list, the things you do like about your current hobbies and leisure activities.

Things I Can Change

A.

B.

Ways to Change Them

A. 1.

2.

3.

B. 1.

2.

3.

Possible Consequences

A. 1.

2.

3.

B. 1.

2.

3.

There is no greater challenge than to have someone relying upon you; no greater satisfaction than to vindicate his expectation.

—KINGMAN BREWSTER

Following is a list of general and specific actions you may want to consider taking. Not everything on the list of suggestions will apply to you nor will they all be right for you. It is hoped, though, that the list will inspire you to come up with your own ideas about how to help yourself, plan for the future, and improve your life. Not forgetting to weigh the risks and consequences, could you see yourself taking any of these actions?

I could subscribe to a magazine.

I could teach someone else my hobby.

I could try to find a new hobby that suits my talents.

I could get more exercise.

I could practice.

I could go to the hobbies section of the library or bookstore.

I could enroll in a course.

I could buy a series of concert, theater, or ballet tickets.

I could do volunteer work.

I could watch less television.

I could try skiing, writing, collecting, painting, drawing, sewing, renovating, playing, building, a new sport, biking, riding, hiking, walking, tennis, chess, a musical instrument, movie-going, sailing, and so on.

I could ____

____

Decision is a risk rooted in the courage of being free.

—PAUL TILLICH

Now it's time to . . .

Act

Look at your new list and ask yourself the following questions:

Which of these things could I do or start doing today?

Which of these things take time?

Are there any first steps I can take today to achieve any of my long-term goals? (For example, if you've decided to take up tennis, today you could find out what courts are available to you.)

What are the general things I will try to do?

Tell yourself, I will do at least one new thing per day until I am satisfied with how I spend my leisure time. I will do everything in my power to work within my limitations. I will try to set realistic goals and will note each accomplishment. I will perceive myself as successful just for trying, and I will be gentle with myself if things do not turn out the way I expect. If I do not accomplish something I have set out to do, I will consider the possibility that I have tried to change something that is not within my power to change, and I will try to learn lessons that will help me in this and other areas of my life. I will not expect to change everything all at once but will take things one step at a time.

THINGS I COULD DO TODAY:	THINGS THAT TAKE TIME:

I WILL DO THE FOLLOWING THINGS TODAY:

EVALUATE

I will keep a list here of all the things I've done and the results I've achieved:

DATE	STEP TAKEN	RESULTS

He who cannot rest, cannot work; he who cannot let go, cannot hold on; he who cannot find footing, cannot go forward.

—HARRY EMERSON FOSDICK

IV.

My Work and School

1. Work
2. Financial Condition
3. School

I. Work

Focus

When I meet somebody new and they ask me, "What do you do?," this is what I tell them:

But there's more to my work than that; this is what I actually and specifically do:

Make two lists side by side (see page 156). On the left, list those things about your work that you feel good about and are satisfied with. On the right, list the things about your work that trouble you or that you would like to improve. Think of everything, general and specific, important and trivial, but circle everything that is very important to you, because these are the things that will deserve special attention later.

Ask yourself any of the following questions that apply to you. If you like, jot down your answers right on the page. Then, later, transfer each answer to whichever list it fits; it's possible that some things will go on both lists.

Do I work too hard, not hard enough, or about the right amount for me?

Do I prefer working for myself or for someone else?

Does it take me very long to get to and from work and do I enjoy the trip?

How are my hours?

Do I like the environment I work in?

Am I comfortable in my workplace?

Do I like the people I work with or for?

Is there autonomy, and is that something I want?

Do I enjoy the routine tasks associated with my work?

Are there special assignments that I particularly enjoy?

Does my work generate feelings of reward and satisfaction or is it just a way to earn money?

Do I earn enough money to suit my needs?

Do I feel underpaid, properly paid, or overpaid?

How is my energy level at work and after work?

Does my work allow for enough leisure time?

Is my work recognized?

Does my work utilize my best talents and skills?

Does my work utilize the talents and skills that I enjoy utilizing?

Are my mind and education being properly utilized?

What are five other specific things about my work that I like and don't like?

Are there any risks associated with this work?

Do I feel secure in my work?

Am I building a successful future, monetarily and otherwise?

Is this something I want to be doing in five years?

Is this something that is leading to what I'd like to be doing in five years?

If and when I retire, would I like it to be from this?

Realistically, how do I see myself in terms of my work one year from now and five years from now?

Is my present course taking me there?

What other issues regarding my work do I want to explore?

Things I Like About My Work:	Things I Don't Like About My Work:

List as many things as possible.

____________________	____________________
____________________	____________________
____________________	____________________
____________________	____________________
____________________	____________________
____________________	____________________
____________________	____________________
____________________	____________________
____________________	____________________
____________________	____________________
____________________	____________________
____________________	____________________
____________________	____________________

Now that you've made two lists, it's time to examine them. First of all, which is longer? Which is longer when you consider only those items that are circled (the things that are important to you)?

If the list of important things you don't like is much longer than the list of things you do like, you might then consider asking yourself whether or not you should begin looking for new work. If the list of things you do like is much longer, you may want to concentrate instead on improving your current work. In either case, it's time to work on changing whichever circled items on the list of things you don't like that are within your control to change.

So that's the next important question to ask yourself: Which items on the list of things I don't like are within my control to change? (It may help to examine the reasons these problems exist in the first place.)

I'm just a plowhand from Arkansas, but I have learned how to hold a team together. How to lift some men up, how to calm down others, until finally they've got one heartbeat, together, a team. There's just three things I ever say. If anything goes bad, then I did it. If anything goes semi-good, then we did it. If anything goes real good, then you did it. That's all it takes to get people to win football games for you.

—BEAR BRYANT

PLAN

What are three things I can do to change each item on the list? List everything now. Later go back and think about the consequences and repercussions of each possible action. Think then, for example, if rectifying a problem will negatively affect any of the things on the other list, the things you do like about your work.

Things I Can Change

A.

B.

Ways to Change Them

A. 1.

2.

3.

B. 1.

2.

3.

Possible Consequences

A. 1.

2.

3.

When I grow up I want to be a little boy.

—JOSEPH HELLER

B. 1.

2.

3.

You must learn day by day, year by year, to broaden your horizon. The more things you love, the more you are interested in, the more you enjoy, the more you are indignant about—the more you have left when anything happens.

—ETHEL BARRYMORE

Following is a list of general and specific actions you may want to consider taking. Not everything on the list of suggestions will apply to you nor will they all be right for you. It is hoped, though, that the list will inspire you to come up with your own ideas about how to help yourself, plan for the future, and improve your life. Not forgetting to weigh the risks and consequences, could you see yourself taking any of these actions?

I could take a class.

I could get up earlier in the morning.

I could dress more professionally.

I could take an evening course.

I could redo my résumé.

I could make a few phone calls.

I could ask for a raise or promotion.

I could work longer or shorter hours.

I could look for a new job in Sunday's paper or on the Internet.

I could get a different job that might lead to the job I want.

I could move to the country or to a new city.

I could ______________________________

____

Take an object. Do something to it. Do something else to it.

—JASPER JOHNS

Now it's time to . . .

ACT

Look at your new list and ask yourself the following questions:

Which of these things could I do or start doing today?

Which of these things take time?

Are there any first steps I can take today to achieve any of my long-term goals? (For example, if you've decided that you may want to go back to school, today you could send away for catalogs.)

What are the general things I will try to do?

Tell yourself, I will do at least one new thing per day until I am satisfied with my work. I will do everything in my power to work within my limitations. I will try to set realistic goals and will note each accomplishment. I will perceive myself as successful just for trying, and I will be gentle with myself if things do not turn out the way I expect. If I do not accomplish something I have set out to do, I will consider the possibility that I have tried to change something that is not within my power to change, and I will try to learn lessons that will help me in this and other areas of my life. I will not expect to change everything all at once but will take things one step at a time.

THINGS I COULD DO TODAY:	THINGS THAT TAKE TIME:

I WILL DO THE FOLLOWING THINGS TODAY:

2. Financial Condition

Focus

This is how I would describe my current financial situation:

____

____

____

____

This is how much money I have:

____

____

____

____

This is a list of my assets:

____

____

____

____

This is how much I think my assets are currently worth:

____

These are my debts (including credit cards):

____

____

____

____

____

This is how much I earn: _______

It is better to have loafed and lost than never to have loafed at all.

—JAMES THURBER

Make two lists side by side (see page 170). On the left, list those things about your financial condition that you are happy about and satisfied with. On the right, list the things about your financial condition that trouble you or that you would like to improve. Think of everything, general and specific, important and trivial, but circle everything that is very important to you, because these are the things that will deserve special attention later.

Ask yourself any of the following questions that apply to you. If you like, jot down your answers right on the page. Then, later, transfer each answer to whichever list it fits; it's possible that some things will go on both lists.

In five years I expect to have saved up________.

In five years I expect to be earning ________.

Am I satisfied with that projection?

Will I need to change my spending habits to achieve that?

Do my spending habits match my spending priorities?

What do I wish I could spend less on?

What expenses can I not rid myself of?

Do I manage my credit cards well?

What might I spend more on?

Do I know how to save money?

Do I have clear-cut financial goals?

If I am saving money, what is it for?

Is my savings invested in a way that makes sense for my financial needs?

Do I wish I could save more money?

How might I cut corners and spend less?

Is there anything I should consider saving for?

Besides cutting corners, are there other ways I might save, such as investing?

Do I know everything I need to or care to know about investing?

Is my financial situation changing, and if so, is it improving or getting worse?

The largest purchase I expect to make over the next five years is _______ .

What financial changes do I expect that are outside my control?

Do I have adequate insurance?

Do I get adequate financial guidance?

Does anyone help me financially, and if there's a risk of losing them, could I rely on myself without them?

Am I happy with my bank?

Can I afford all of the things I want?

Do I expect to be able to afford all of the things I want over the next five years?

Do I think I could benefit from being on a budget?

How strict a budget could I live with?

Do I live within my means or above my means?

Do people call me a spendthrift or a cheapskate or a wise investor?

Do I agree with them, and if so, would I like to change that?

What are my feelings and attitudes about money?

Do I lie about money—to myself or others?

Am I proud of any financial accomplishments?

Have I made any great financial mistakes? If so, am I happy with how I handled the results?

Do I seem to learn from my financial mistakes?

Am I generous, too generous, or not generous enough?

Has anyone stolen from me, and, if so, has this affected my attitudes about money?

Am I jealous of people who have more than I?

Am I satisfied with my financial situation?

Am I afraid of losing what I have?

Do I work too hard for my money, not hard enough, or about right for me?

The best thing about my financial situation is __________.

The thing about my financial situation that worries me most or has me the most dissatisfied is __________ .

How do I think people get rich?

Am I rich?

Do I want to be rich?

How much is rich for me?

Realistically, how do I see myself in terms of my finances one year from now and five years from now?

Is my present course taking me there?

What other issues regarding my finances do I want to explore?

For fast-acting relief, try slowing down.

—LILY TOMLIN

Things I Like About My Financial Condition:	Things I Don't Like About My Financial Condition:

List as many things as possible.

Now that you've made two lists, it's time to examine them. First of all, which is longer? Which is longer when you consider only those items that are circled (the things that are important to you)?

If the list of important things you don't like is much longer than the list of things you do like, you might then consider asking yourself whether or not you should concentrate on changing your financial outlook and goals. If the list of things you do like is much longer, you might then consider continuing along your current course. In either case, it's time to work on changing whichever circled items on the list of things you don't like that are within your control to change.

So that's the next important question to ask yourself: Which items on the list of things I don't like that are within my control to change? (It may help to examine the reasons these problems exist in the first place.)

When in charge, ponder. When in trouble, delegate. When in doubt, mumble.

—Good Life Almanac

PLAN

What are three things I can do to change each item on the list? List everything now. Later go back and think about the consequences and repercussions of each possible action. Think then, for example, if rectifying a problem will negatively affect any of the things on the other list, the things you do like about your financial condition.

Things I Can Change

A.

B.

Ways to Change Them

A. 1.

2.

3.

B. 1.

2.

3.

Possible Consequences

A. 1.

2.

3.

Life is short; live it up.

—NIKITA S. KHRUSHCHEV

B. 1.

2.

3.

If you doubt you can accomplish something, then you can't accomplish it. You have to have confidence in your ability, and then be tough enough to follow through.

—ROSALYNN CARTER

Following is a list of general and specific actions you may want to consider taking. Not everything on the list of suggestions will apply to you nor will they all be right for you. It is hoped, though, that the list will inspire you to come up with your own ideas about how to help yourself, plan for the future, and improve your life. Not forgetting to weigh the risks and consequences, could you see yourself taking any of these actions?

I could subscribe to a business magazine.

I could get a financial advisor.

I could start a budget.

I could ask for a raise.

I could take a course in investing or read a book on the subject.

I could start my own business.

I could change my business or streamline it.

I could practice or develop a new skill.

I could do some temp work.

I could try safer or riskier investment.

I could deposit a set amount of money into the bank each month.

I could ____

____

We must learn to be still in the midst of activity and to be vibrantly alive in repose.

—Indira Gandhi

Now it's time to . . .

ACT

Look at your new list and ask yourself the following questions:

Which of these things could I do or start doing today?

Which of these things take time?

Are there any first steps I can take today to achieve any of my long-term goals? (For example, if you've decided to go on a budget but don't know where to begin, today you could buy a home budget book.)

What are the general things I will try to do?

Tell yourself, I will do at least one new thing per day until I am satisfied with the state of my financial condition. I will do everything in my power to work within my limitations. I will try to set realistic goals and will note each accomplishment. I will perceive myself as successful just for trying, and I will be gentle with myself if things do not turn out the way I expect. If I do not accomplish something I have set out to do, I will consider the possibility that I have tried to change something that is not within my power to change, and I will try to learn lessons that will help me in this and other areas of my life. I will not expect to change everything all at once but will take things one step at a time.

Things I Could Do Today:	Things That Take Time:

I will do the following things today:

3. School

Focus

When people ask me, "How's school?" or "What are you studying?," this is what I say:

This is how I really feel about school and being a student:

This is how I spend a typical day:

____

____

____

____

Make two lists side by side (see page 182). On the left, list those things about being a student in school that you feel good about and are satisfied with. On the right, list the things about school that trouble you or that you would like to improve. Think of everything, general and specific, important and trivial, but circle everything that is very important to you, because these are the things that will deserve special attention later.

Ask yourself any of the following questions that apply to you. If you like, jot down your answers right on the page. Then, later, transfer each answer to whichever list it fits; it's possible that some things will go on both lists.

What are the worst things about being in school?

What are the best things about being in school?

Do I get enough physical exercise?

Do I feel relaxed or wound up most of the time?

Do I get enough sleep?

Do I have good study habits?

Am I satisfied with my grades?

Am I satisfied with the level of education?

Do I like my teachers?

Do I get enough leisure time?

Am I satisfied with my financial situation?

Is this a good school for me?

Am I learning what I came to school to learn?

Will this experience help me achieve my goals later?

What are my talents and skills?

Of those, which do I enjoy using the most?

Does my school or my life outside of school allow me to practice or improve those talents and skills?

Do I know what's available at my school and am I making use of its resources?

Am I satisfied with my living situation?

Is my environment conducive to studying?

Is it easy enough for me to get to my classes?

Do I have the proper tools to study with?

Do I have any limitations that make it hard to study?

Am I satisfied with my social life?

Do I have enough time to do what's important to me?

Is drug and alcohol use prevalent at my school, and is this an issue for me in any way?

Can I pinpoint the problems in my life?

Am I under excessive pressure?

Do I pressure myself to achieve or does my family pressure me?

Do my problems interfere with my studies?

What do I hope to have gotten out of my education over the next five years?

Realistically, how do I see myself in terms of school one year from now and five years from now?

Is my present course taking me there?

What other issues regarding my school do I want to explore?

Luck? I don't know anything about luck. I've never banked on it, and I'm afraid of people who do. Luck to me is something else: hard work—and realizing what is opportunity and what isn't.

—LUCILLE BALL

THINGS I LIKE ABOUT SCHOOL:	THINGS I DON'T LIKE ABOUT SCHOOL:

List as many things as possible.

______________________	______________________
______________________	______________________
______________________	______________________
______________________	______________________
______________________	______________________
______________________	______________________
______________________	______________________
______________________	______________________
______________________	______________________
______________________	______________________
______________________	______________________
______________________	______________________
______________________	______________________

Now that you've made two lists, it's time to examine them. First of all, which is longer? Which is longer when you consider only those items that are circled (the things that are important to you)?

If the list of important things you don't like is much longer than the list of things you do like, you might then consider asking yourself whether or not, if possible, you should consider not being a student or changing schools. If the list of things you do like is much longer, you might want to concentrate instead on improving your life as a student. In either case, it's time to work on changing whichever circled items on the list of things you don't like that are within your control to change.

So that's the next important question to ask yourself: Which items on the list of things I don't like are within my control to change? (It may help to examine the reasons these problems exist in the first place.)

The one important thing I have learned over the years is the difference between taking one's work seriously and taking one's self seriously. The first is imperative and the second is disastrous.

—MARGOT FONTEYN

Plan

What are three things I can do to change each item on the list? List everything now. Later go back and think about the consequences and repercussions of each possible action. Think then, for example, if rectifying a problem will negatively affect any of the things on the other list, the things you do like about being a student.

Things I Can Change

A.

B.

Ways to Change Them

A. 1.

2.

3.

B. 1.

2.

3.

Possible Consequences

A. 1.

2.

3.

I've never been poor, only broke. Being poor is a frame of mind. Being broke is only a temporary situation.

—MIKE TODD

B. 1.

2.

3.

Never underestimate the value of luck, but remember that luck comes to those searching for something.

—STANLEY MARCUS

Following is a list of general and specific actions you may want to consider taking. Not everything on the list of suggestions will apply to you nor will they all be right for you. It is hoped, though, that the list will inspire you to come up with your own ideas about how to help yourself, plan for the future, and improve your life. Not forgetting to weigh the risks and consequences, could you see yourself taking any of these actions?

I could study harder or not quite so hard.

I could join some clubs.

I could find new ways to relax (yoga, meditation, poetry, concerts).

I could choose different courses.

I could research scholarship opportunities.

I could do more/less with my roommate or get a new one.

I could plan my time better so that I don't have to stay up all night.

I could change my major.

I could form a study group.

I could ______________________________

____

Never continue in a job you don't enjoy. If you're happy in what you're doing, you'll like yourself, you'll have inner peace. And if you have that, along with physical health, you will have had more success than you could possibly have imagined.

—Johnny Carson

Now it's time to . . .

ACT

Look at your new list and ask yourself the following questions:

Which of these things could I do or start doing today?

Which of these things take time?

Are there any first steps I can take today to achieve any of my long-term goals? (For example, if you've decided to improve your grade in chemistry, today you could read the next chapter in your textbook.)

What are the general things I will try to do?

Tell yourself, I will do at least one new thing per day until I am satisfied with my school life. I will do everything in my power to work within my limitations. I will try to set realistic goals and will note each accomplishment. I will perceive myself as successful just for trying, and I will be gentle with myself if things do not turn out the way I expect. If I do not accomplish something I have set out to do, I will consider the possibility that I have tried to change something that is not within my power to change, and I will try to learn lessons that will help me in this and other areas of my life. I will not expect to change everything all at once but will take things one step at a time.

THINGS I COULD DO TODAY:	THINGS THAT TAKE TIME:

I WILL DO THE FOLLOWING THINGS TODAY:

EVALUATE

I will keep a list here of all the things I've done and the results I've achieved:

DATE	STEP TAKEN	RESULTS

V.

Here I Am Again

Building on My Experience Up Until Now

1. What I've Learned About What's Possible for Me: A Checklist of Changes I've Made
2. The Pep Talk I Want to Give Myself: Things I Still Need to Work On
3. Moving Right Along: The Next Challenge

1. What I've Learned About What's Possible for Me

A Checklist of Changes I've Made

Look over your evaluations at the end of each part you have worked on and try to summarize: Think of the best changes and plans you made, your major accomplishments, things that didn't work out so well, things you'd like to do more of, things you'd like to do in addition. Don't forget to look at the risks you took and how they worked out and any possible negative consequences that you'd like to avoid in the future.

The following are highlights of the things I've done and the results I've achieved:

HEALTH

DATE	STEP TAKEN	RESULTS

Family and Relationships

Date	Step Taken	Results

HOME AND COMMUNITY

DATE	STEP TAKEN	RESULTS

WORK AND SCHOOL

DATE	STEP TAKEN	RESULTS

OTHER

DATE	STEP TAKEN	RESULTS

2. The Pep Talk I Want to Give Myself

Things I Still Need to Work On

If you're having trouble getting started, begin by thumbing through this book—your book. Evaluate your progress. Read the quotes that are sprinkled throughout the book. Circle the ones that inspire you. Incorporate those sentiments into your pep talk. Be positive. Why are you terrific? List all of your best qualities. How can you be even better? If you could have anything in the world, what things would you want? What would make you feel great? How are you going to get some of those things?

Use the techniques you've learned in this book to work further on those areas of your life that you have chosen to focus on or come up with some new ones.

A list of plans I'd like to make and issues I'd like to resolve:

3. Moving Right Along

The Next Challenge

Using the techniques you've learned in this book, choose a subject of concern to you and tailor-make your own five-year plan.

All prosperity begins in the mind and is dependent only upon the full use of our creative imagination.

—RUTH ROSS, PH.D.

FOCUS

Plan

ACT

EVALUATE